STUMPED

The Legacy of the Great Pine Harvest in Mid-Michigan

Cover Photo Credit: On the sleigh haul. Doubling up over the hill. Photographer, Albert J. Bradshaw, Oscoda, Michigan, circa 1910.

Published by Mission Point Press
2554 Chandler Rd.
Traverse City, MI 49696
(231) 421-9513
www.MissionPointPress.com

Design by Sarah Meiers

ISBN 978-1-961302-10-5
Library of Congress Control Number 2023912875

Printed in the United States of America

STUMPED

The Legacy of the Great Pine Harvest
in Mid-Michigan

THOMAS A. SCHUPBACH

MISSION POINT PRESS

To Sophia and Julianne, had they lived.

TABLE OF CONTENTS

FOREWORD

S
tumped: The Legacy of the Great Pine Harvest in Mid-Michigan, a historical account of early logging in West Nester Township of Roscommon County, Michigan, written by Thomas Schupbach, is a delightful read for anyone interested in learning more about Michigan's short but colorful "White Pine Era" of logging.

This book provides a valuable addition to the history of early settlement, logging and railroad development in north-central Michigan. Lumber barons, loggers, railroad and sawmill owners, woods workers, sportsmen, city-dwelling investors, school teachers, and farmers all take their place in this well-researched and fascinating account of the boom and bust of Michigan's early logging. Schupbach's book shows us in its real-life episodes that most of Michigan in the late 1800's was still a rough and tumble wilderness just on the cusp of being settled.

Official records of land transactions were brief or non-existent in most parts of Michigan. But here, in West Nester Township many records were, for various reasons, preserved. Through his thorough research, the writer allows us to read an accurate accounting of land ownerships and the backgrounds and history of the various owners and players involved with the early lumbering of West Nester Township.

Place names and towns that no longer exist, names of towns that were changed to those we are familiar with today are mentioned along with maps of where old railroads and new towns and villages sprang up make this book especially interesting and different from many other books dealing with this subject.

A good read indeed!

Keith R. Martell Jr.
Consultant Forester, Gaylord, Mich.

INTRODUCTION

L
ook on any map of Roscommon County, Michigan, that delineates state and private land and one striking feature of the southeast corner of the county is the nearly perfect inholding formed by the western half of Nester Township, a single surveyed township. Three sides of this township are surrounded by state land. This is in stark contrast to what is typically seen throughout the state, a seemingly random interspersed mix of state and private property. This anomaly has deep roots that date back to the turn of the century, but the township has a substantial history that predates even this peculiarity.

Nester Township, like many rural areas of the northern portion of the state, has a dearth of recorded local history. This is typical of the large areas of cutover land found in northern Michigan. With no continuum of occupation, from the lumber era through the attempts at agriculture or the abandonment of the land to the state, it is no surprise that little history was recorded or passed down. The players moved on after the lumber harvest. The stories vanished as swiftly as had the virgin forest.

As early as 1969, Dr. John Porter, when compiling a history of Mid-Forest Lodge, remarked that the township history prior to 1900 "seems unavailable" for he had been unable "to make any contacts in that direction." He can be excused, for there was little oral history, few township records, no enduring settlements, or any known epistolary collections.[1]

Likewise, there are no known Native American records or sites in the township, though the Grand Traverse, Saginaw Trail did cut the extreme southwest corner of the township. But within the county, especially around Houghton Lake, there were located several mounds, villages, and burial grounds. Undoubtedly, the township was utilized by native people but perhaps only for seasonal hunting and fishing.[2]

It may seem incongruous that a surveyed township is worthy of a separate historical treatment. Certainly, it is small history, but with surprising breadth. It comprises three separate railroad systems and would exemplify the era of large land transactions, an era which would be unusually prolonged in the county into the 1930s. It is a story both notable and peculiar. And though not filled with large historic figures, it is fascinating nonetheless.

Nester Township encompasses two surveyed townships, and this brief chronicle focuses primarily on the western surveyed township, referred to as West Nester Township.

West Nester Township is cut, roughly diagonally, from the southwest to the northeast by a glacial moraine, making it some of the higher ground in the county. The dividing line between two important river drainages, the Tittabawassee and the Muskegon, closely follows this same diagonal and would have ramifications on the lumbermen that came to this township seeking out the great pine forests found in its highlands.

These lumbermen brought the full force of the 19th century's industrial might to the area. Their railroad network would have provided the conduits for timber too inaccessible to be harvested economically by simple hauling to a requisite stream. This network also exposed the township to the full tumult of America's insatiable need for lumber.

Never again would this land be the large-scale focus of one era's foremost commercial enterprise. During the late 1800s, this enterprise arrived solely to withdraw hundreds of years of reserves from a biological bank account that had accumulated since the glaciers retreated.

The township's story, though, would continue beyond the lumber era and include a noteworthy attempt at converting the cutover land to agriculture and the eventual formation of a renowned sportsman's club.

All these early efforts to grapple a livelihood from West Nester left fading marks on this landscape. Still commonplace today, the old railroad beds, pine stumps, lake pilings and farm fields all hint at the aspirations of these forgotten individuals. This subtle heritage is still an alluring link to the past for all those familiar with the township.

CHAPTER 1

"The Water Pure and Deep"

Their bearing is north, setting the dividing line between townships 21 north and range 1 and 2 west of Michigan's principal meridian, roughly following present day F-97 in southern Roscommon County. John Brink, deputy surveyor, heads the small survey crew. It is April, a normally propitious month for survey work due to the lack of insect pests, obstructive vegetation (green-up does not occur until May), and extreme weather. Yet Brink, although inured to the hardships of survey work, is hindered by snow, and bemoans that it is "two and half feet deep and is hard getting along" as they proceed along the east side of sections 24 and 13. Here the day's work would end.[1]

Brink had come to Michigan to survey "a strip of land 150 miles long and twenty-four miles wide into townships." Reflecting on his seven years of government survey work, he described a typical surveying party as "two chainmen, an axe man, a cook, a packman and myself." Survey expeditions "would last from five to eleven months." It was grueling work demanding a tolerance for deprivation. Arriving in camp, he recalled being "ready to eat our supper and lay down and sleep." There was "no time to sit around a camp fire and dry wet clothes." To Brink, going "three months at a time without having all my clothes dry" was no exaggeration. Nor was it unusual to "wade through miles of swamp" or "swim streams with the ice running."[2]

Continuing his work along the east edge of section 12 on April 11, 1837, just months after Michigan was granted statehood, the crew would play out the chains, 80 to the mile, and at 52.77 chains, they would intersect the south margin of an unnamed lake. With accuracy amazing for its time, they recorded 79.38 chains over the lake and set the section corner (80 chains) on the north shore. It is doubtful if John Brink would long remember this body of water but in his survey notes there is a rare yet notable aside of it "having high banks, the water pure and deep." Here was the earliest recorded mention of what would eventually be called Clear Lake. Coincidence alone allowed for this early visit by Brink, for the lake was fortuitously situated on a township line.[3]

Brink would go on to survey the rest of the township border of West Nester, commenting on the soils and vegetation. In May, working west, setting the southern boundary, he passed through a burnt-over tract (section 36) with much of the timber down and by the time he reached section 31, he harshly summarized the terrain, stating, "I can say nothing in favor of this country as yet." The west boundary work was performed this same month, but the northern border would not be surveyed until May 1838 when the township boundary work was finished.[4]

The section lines dividing the township would not be finalized until September 1850. This time, the famous surveyor William Burt, inventor of the solar compass and discoverer of iron ore in Michigan, was requested to resurvey after the fraudulent work performed by an earlier surveyor (not Brink) of the section lines. Burt commented on the soil, topography, and timber, but also exclaimed that the "lakes and small streams afford good water."[5] [6]

John Brink (1811–1904)

Image courtesy of the McHenry County Historical Society & Museum.
John Brink was 26 years old when he surveyed the township lines
in Roscommon County. He was 88 when he recounted some of his
experiences to the *Milwaukee Sentinel* in 1899. It is believed this photo
was taken that same year.

CHAPTER 2

A Land-Office Business

B y the 1860s, the lands in Roscommon County, being part of the public domain, were subject to a variety of federal programs that provided for their transfer to private ownership. In West Nester Township, the land was disbursed under several of these programs, generally identified as the following: cash purchase, railroad land grants, War of 1812 warrants, swamp land grants, agriculture script, military bounty land warrants and homesteading. All but 480 acres were transferred to private ownership from 1860 to 1873.

The map and legend on the following pages summarize the original owners of land patents in West Nester Township. Surprisingly, for the whole township there were only 25 unique purchasers, which ranged from large corporations to individual homesteaders. The accompanying legend identifies the owners (in descending order based on total acreage), the total acreage of each owner, the type of entry/entries utilized by each owner and the year(s) of entry.

These first patentees for much of Roscommon County were mostly speculative investors, many from Michigan. Also included were several lumbermen, though only one was known to have actually operated in the township. The most notable and largest acquirer was the Amboy, Lansing & Traverse Bay Railroad Company.

Map showing by colors and numbers the original patentees for West Nester Township. The legend is on the following page.

Map Color/#	Original Purchaser	Approx Acreage	Type of Entry	Year
	Amboy, Lansing & Traverse Bay RR Co.	11,000	R R Land Grant	1861
	George S. Frost	4,280	War of 1812 Warrants	1866
	Jefferson F. Bundy & John G. Lowman	1,520	War of 1812 Warrants	1866
			Cash	1866
	Emma Ripley	1,160	War of 1812 Warrants	1866
			War of 1812 Warrants	1869
			War of 1812 Warrants	1870
			Swamp Land Grant	1866
			Agr. Script	1866
	Charles L. Ortman & Sigmund Rothschild	960	Cash	1871
			Cash	1872
			War of 1812 Warrants	1871
			Mil. Bounty Land Warrant	1872
			Swamp Land Grant	1873
	Schmemann, Ortmann & Böing	880	Cash	1872
			Cash	1873
	Eber B. Ward	400	Cash	1860
	Stephen M. Shurtleff	360	Swamp Land Grant	1870
	William P. Irwin	360	War of 1812 Warrants	1871
			Cash	1871
	Josiah W. Begole	360	War of 1812 Warrants	1871
1	James A. & David F. Irwin	280	Cash	1868
2	William Rogers	200	War of 1812 Warrants	1869
3	David G. Wilcox & Jacob Snyder	160	Cash	1869
4	Wilson (Wm. Hotchkiss, Farwell A., & Wm. Henry)	160	Cash	1884
5	A. W. Heather & J. A. Irwin	160	War of 1812 Warrants	1868
6	John Owen	160	Swamp Land Grant	1872
7	Catherine McBain	160	Cash	1872
8	William H. Weaver	160	Homestead	1886*
9	Benjamin Hartshorn	80	Cash	1868
10	Charles W. Wells	40	Cash	1884
11	Charles L. Ortman	40	Swamp Land Grant	1873
12	John J. Rupp & Addison P. Brewer	40	Cash	1882
13	Samuel Medbury	40	Cash	1869
14	Maurice Quinn	40	Cash	1881
15	Rory McLeod	40	Homestead	1887**

*Final proof 1893
**Final proof 1894

Ultimately, what primarily drove these purchases and speculation was the quantity and quality of the standing white pine.

Aside from the railroad land grantee, what most of these original individual landowners shared was a level of economic success that provided them with investment capital. Pinelands were a commodity to speculate on, an investment such that with the growing demand and shrinking local supply, money could be made by holding these properties right up until they were sold to the actual lumbermen who would harvest the specific tract. Below is a brief background of each of the patentees.

As stated, the owner of the largest amount of acreage in the township was the Amboy, Lansing & Traverse Bay Railroad Company. In 1856, Congress granted Michigan land to aid in the construction of certain railroads. These railroads could claim land along the route of the proposed tracks, originally within six miles of the route with an indemnity limit of fifteen miles. Because the original proposed route was to terminate at Traverse Bay and its path was significantly west of the eventual railroad itself (which terminated in Mackinaw City), all of West Nester Township fell within this 15-mile limit. This explains why the extreme southwest corner of the township, which fell outside of a 15-mile limit from the actual path of the railroad, could be claimed under this land grant.[1]

The claimed railroad lands were also limited to every other section within the allowed strip of land. Within West Nester Township this pattern of odd-numbered sections is seen on the map on page 6. The Amboy, Lansing & Traverse Bay Railroad Company claimed approximately 11,000 acres within the township, or approximately 47.7% of the township. The Jackson, Lansing & Saginaw Railroad Company purchased the Amboy, Lansing & Traverse Bay Railroad Company and its land grant in 1866. In 1871, the Jackson, Lansing & Saginaw Railroad Company came under the control of the Michigan Central Railroad.

George S. Frost (1824–1890) was a boy when his family moved from New York to Pontiac. He soon began an early career clerking in Pontiac, Troy, and finally, Detroit. It was in Detroit that he came under the guidance and friendship of General Lewis Cass. General Cass assisted the young man in beginning his career in the Surveyor-General office. This experience led to a position as Land Commissioner of the Saint Mary's Falls Ship Canal Company. He eventually began his own business buying and selling pinelands. He was ultimately credited with selling "more land than any other person in Michigan." Frost procured more acres in West Nester Township than any other individual or group of buyers, acquiring over 4,000 acres in 1866.[2]

John G. Lowman (1826–1910) and Jefferson F. Bundy (1824–1874) were partners in a Saginaw Valley lumber mill during the mid-1860s. As partners, they purchased approximately 1,520 acres in West Nester Township. Lowman was from Chemung, New York, and after achieving success in the lumber business in Michigan, sold out his interest and eventually returned to Chemung. Bundy was also born in New York but remained in Saginaw until his death in 1874.[3][4]

As the wife of the one-time register of the United States Land Office in East Saginaw, Emma Ripley (1835–1902) accumulated over 1,000 acres in West Nester Township. Some of these lands were accumulated while her husband, Henry Clay Ripley (1831–1904), held that office. Over his career in Saginaw, Henry was a collector of internal revenue, a lumberman, and a real estate dealer. Perhaps it was because of his office and a perceived conflict of interest that the lands were placed in her name. Regardless, Emma was one of only two women listed as an original patentee.[5]

Charles L. Ortmann (1830–1897) came to East Saginaw from Austria in 1864. His early career in Europe was in the mercantile trade. Once in Michigan, he engaged in the logging and lumber business. Charles quickly established himself in East Saginaw helping found the East Saginaw Savings Bank and was even elected mayor of East Saginaw in 1872. Eventually, he moved to Detroit and was involved in the paper and chemical industries. Charles and Sigmund Rothschild (1837–1907) purchased almost 1,000 acres in West Nester Township. Rothschild was a German by birth who immigrated to the United States in 1853. Settling in Detroit the following year, he embarked on a career in the tobacco industry, achieving great success establishing a wholesale tobacco house. He bought extensive pinelands in Michigan. Charles also purchased 40 additional acres on his own.[6][7]

Karl Schmemann (1842–1899) was no stranger to the intricacies of the United States Land Office. Soon after immigrating to the United States, he accepted a position as clerk in the Detroit Office. It was in the insurance business, though, that he spent the bulk of his career, working first for the Buffalo German Insurance Company, then the St. Paul German Insurance Company and, finally, the Milwaukee Mechanics Insurance Company.

Wilhelm Böing (1846–1890) arrived in the United States in 1868 having emigrated from Westphalia in the Kingdom of Prussia (part of the German Empire). Böing settled in Detroit and Americanized his name to Boeing. He quickly advanced economically, finding employment with Charles Ortmann in Saginaw. Wilhelm began buying timberlands in Michigan as early as 1872. This rapidly led to a career in lumbering, real estate, and iron ore. Wilhelm married Charles Ortmann's daughter, Marie, and fathered a son, William Edward (1881–1956). The son, benefiting from his father's Michigan fortune, founded the aircraft company bearing their name. Schmemann, Ortmann and Boeing purchased 880 acres of pineland in West Nester Township in 1872–3.[8]

Eber Brock Ward (1811–1875) became one of the wealthiest men in Michigan by the time of his death. He began his remarkable career on the Great Lakes during the age of the lake schooners. He transitioned to steam navigation, commanding vessels and investing in the industry. Eventually, with the rise of the railroads, he focused on the iron and railroad business, as well as glass manufacturing and silver mining. Besides these interests, Ward purchased thousands of acres of pinelands in Michigan and Wisconsin, including 400 acres in West Nester Township in 1860.[9]

Three hundred and sixty acres of land in West Nester were recorded as purchased by Stephen Miles Shurtleff (1817–1869) in July of 1870. Shurtleff was a lawyer originally from New York who died in 1869 in Niles, Michigan. How these acres were recorded, apparently posthumously, is unclear.

William Patton Irwin (1833–1876) was a successful grain merchant from upstate New York. "He was largely interested in real estate having important holdings in Michigan, South Carolina, New York City, Brooklyn, Albany, and Greenbush. At the time of his death, he was the president of the East Albany Banking and Trust Company, and a prominent member of the Albany Board of Trade." His Michigan holdings included 360 acres in West Nester Township.[10]

When he arrived in Genesee County in 1836 it was still a largely unbroken wilderness. By 1883, he was governor of Michigan. Josiah William Begole (1815–1896) came alone to Michigan from New York with $100 in his pocket, intent on settling in this virgin land. Besides developing a farm of 500 acres, he became involved in all levels of government. He was, at various times, a school inspector, Justice of the Peace, county treasurer, state senator, federal congressman and, ultimately, a one-term governor. While in the state senate in 1871 he purchased 360 acres in West Nester Township.[11]

James A. Irwin and David F. Irwin purchased 280 acres in West Nester during 1868. At the time of purchase, they were residents of Clearfield County, Pennsylvania.

Rogers City, in Presque Isle County, Michigan, is named after William Evans Rogers (1846–1913) who purchased hundreds of acres in that county as he partnered with Albert Molitor in the lumber business. Rogers was a lieutenant of the United States Engineer Corps, stationed in Detroit from 1867–69, and he surveyed portions of the Lake Superior shore and Lake St. Clair. A lawyer and engineer, he spent the rest of his career in New York in the railroad industry and in private law practice. He also purchased 200 acres in West Nester Township in 1869.[12]

The lumbering firm known as the Wilson Brothers was actually made up of two brothers and a cousin. The brothers were William Hotchkiss Wilson (1839–1914) and Farwell Alonzo Wilson (1841–1896) and they had begun their business in 1866. Their cousin William Henry Wilson (1846–1914) joined them in 1868. The Wilsons initially operated in Isabella County but were most noted for establishing their mill and store in the new town of Harrison in 1880. They operated in Harrison until the mid 1890s. The Wilsons donated the original site of their mill to the city. Today it is Wilson State Park on Budd Lake. In 1884, the firm purchased 160 acres in West Nester Township.[13]

Alexander W. Heather (1832–1906) was a land speculator from Saginaw. He partnered with J. A. Irwin, also from Saginaw, and purchased 160 acres in West Nester Township in 1868.

Born in England, John G. Owen (1824–1901) came to Armada, Macomb County, Michigan, in 1843 and began a varied and successful series of careers. These included farmer, clerk, proprietor of a mercantile business, grain mill owner and dealer in wholesale groceries and lumbermen's supplies. He was also a lumber manufacturer, lumber mill owner, state senator and mayor of East Saginaw. The town of Owendale in Huron County is named after him. It was there that he had purchased an extensive tract of land for timber and eventually agriculture. In 1872, while a mill owner in Saginaw, he purchased 160 acres in West Nester Township.[14] [15]

Catherine McBain (born 1840–1 in Scotland) was the wife of William McBain (1823–1894). They emigrated from Canada to East Saginaw in 1867 where William became involved in the grocery and lumber business. In 1880, William began a new career in the insurance business. The William McBain & Son insurance firm became one of the largest in the Saginaws. During 1872, Catherine purchased hundreds of acres of pineland in Michigan, including 160 acres in West Nester Township.[16] [17]

In 1886, William H. Weaver selected 160 acres in section 36 of West Nester Township to homestead. He had proved up this land by 1893 and was granted a patent on February 10, 1894. Weaver would remain in Nester Township until the fall of 1896 when he moved to the Breckenridge area of Gratiot County.[18]

Like James A. and David F. Irwin, Benjamin Hartshorn (1833–1916) was from Clearfield County, Pennsylvania. Benjamin never married and was a Pennsylvania farmer his whole life. He purchased 80 acres. It is unclear why several citizens of Clearfield County, Pennsylvania, invested in West Nester Township in 1868. Since both the Irwin and Hartshorn purchases were in section 16 (the school section as defined by the Land Ordinance of 1785), perhaps these school sections were promoted for sale more widely and via different avenues throughout the United States.[19]

One original patentee in the township, who was also one of the lumbermen to ultimately operate within the township, was Charles William Wells (1841–1893). After serving in a New York Infantry Company during the Civil War, Charles Wells came to Saginaw in 1867. His career in Michigan began in the lumbermen's supply business. By 1868 he was partnered with Farnum C. Stone and Ammi W. Wright in the firm Wells, Stone & Company. The "principal business of the company was that of wholesale grocers, but gradually there was added the trading in pine lands, logs and lumber." Mr. Wells was allied with Thomas Nester in the early lumber development in the southern West Nester Township. He purchased one of the last 40 acres in West Nester Township in 1884.[20]

John J. Rupp (1847–1927) had various interests in the Saginaw valley after arriving there in 1855. He was the first vice-president of the board of trade, board member of the Saginaw Plate Glass Company, president of the People's Savings Bank and a lumberman for much of his life. Addison P. Brewer (1826–1905) came with his family in 1833 from the Catskills to Oakland County, Michigan. Trained as a teacher, he was lured away from that career to become a chainman on a surveying crew in the Upper Peninsula. His experience led to a full-time career surveying. By 1859, he was appointed a State Swamp Road commissioner, which brought him to East Saginaw and to a future as a lumberman, mill owner, and dealer in pinelands. Rupp and Brewer purchased 40 acres in West Nester Township in 1882.[21]

Arriving in Detroit from New York in 1857, Samuel Medbury (1808–1874) set about managing the Peninsular Bank and overseeing his various business interests in Michigan. He later would become prominent in the State Bank of Michigan and partner in the tobacco trade. Eventually he would focus solely on his real estate business, "embracing city property, pine-lands, and farms in various portions of Michigan and other States." Five years before his death in 1869, he purchased 40 acres in West Nester Township.[22]

At the age of 18, Maurice Quinn (1844–1913) left Quebec, the province of his birth, and came to Saginaw. He originally worked on a railroad construction crew before becoming a railroad contractor. After a short stint lumbering, he spent the rest of his career dealing in pinelands throughout the United States and Canada. He purchased 40 acres in West Nester Township in 1881.[23]

Many of the shanty boys that came to Michigan hailed from Canada, and Rory Mcleod was one of them. In 1880, he was working in a camp in Gerrish Township, Roscommon County. By 1887, he was the second of only two individuals to file a homestead claim in West Nester Township. Rory would prove up his 40-acre claim in 1894.[24]

CHAPTER 3

The Road to Houghton Lake

I t was the first internal improvement in Roscommon County, penetrating the county before the Ionia and Houghton Lake State Road, the Tawas and Manistee State Road or the Jackson, Lansing & Saginaw Railroad. It became the first legitimate avenue for settlers to reach Houghton Lake and for lumbermen to tote supplies to the vast pinelands just being targeted for harvest.

Referred to as the Midland, Houghton Lake & Traverse Bay State Road it would transect Roscommon County roughly from the southeast to the northwest. Michigan Act 176, authorizing this road, was signed into law in March of 1863. The act sought to "provide for the drainage and reclaimation [sic] of swamp land by means of a State road and ditches, from Midland City to Grand Traverse Bay." The road would be funded by appropriating 640 acres of state swamp land per mile of road constructed. Contracts for the construction of the road were not immediately forthcoming, perhaps in part due to the Civil War, but additionally because the appropriation was apparently insufficient. To remedy this, the legislature, in March of 1867, enhanced the appropriation by adding an additional 640 acres of state swamp land per mile.[1][2]

This augmentation must have been successful for, by the summer of 1868, work was proceeding. Contracts had been let for most of its length. The job was split into two divisions: The eastern division that would construct the road from Midland to Houghton Lake and the western division that would build from Traverse Bay to Houghton Lake. The eastern section would connect Midland and Houghton Lake, following a path to "Red Keg" (Averill's), Edenville, Burt's farm (several miles north of Gladwin) and then five miles along the western border of West Nester Township before angling to Houghton Lake.[3]

The eastern division was surveyed by Perley Heald of Midland and was 60.75 miles long. Contracts for the last 24.75 miles originally went to Mr. William Scott but were later sold to John Owens and Addison Brewer of Saginaw, who sublet the contract for ten miles to John Kilbourne of Zilwaukee.[4]

Relying on the survey books of Perley Heald and John Owens's travels over the road, the *Saginaw Enterprise* provided the following description of the last 24 miles of this nascent roadway in 1868. From "Burt's farm to the forty-eighth mile, a distance of twelve miles, the land is covered with pine. It is rolling, and is good farming land. From the forty-eighth mile to the lake the land has been burnt over, and consequently the timber is not heavy."[5]

The *Saginaw Enterprise*, understanding how uninformed its city, especially its business community, was about the road, claimed that very "few of our business men, perhaps, appreciate the results which will attend the completion of this new State Road." Further, regarding the difficulty of delivering supplies to the lumber camps in this region, the *Enterprise* claimed that the "new State Road will revolutionize all of this vast trade." Now "lumberman *[sic]* will find it very greatly to their advantage to purchase supplies here (Saginaw), ship them by rail to Averills and thence by a good State road to the lumber camps."[6]

By the spring of 1869, the road was "chopped" out from Burt's farm above Gladwin to Houghton Lake. Though construction was expedited by the fact that little grading or ditching was required, this wagon road was still only predicted to reach Houghton Lake by July. Even then, settlers were already utilizing this rough-hewn road and locating along it, especially near Houghton Lake.[7]

As true today as then, the timeframe for the culmination of public-works projects could often be unduly optimistic. In June, the completion of the road was expected to be in the fall of 1869. By September, however, hoping now to be finished by winter, 120 men were employed pushing to add to the 40 miles already completed on the western division. On the eastern division, the road east of Houghton Lake for 24 miles was expected to be done by winter, leaving only eight or ten miles unfinished.[8] [9] [10]

An end-of-year summary for 1869 now predicted that the contracts would be finished in 1870. On the western division, settlers were "now to be found on the line of the road nearly 40 miles" from Traverse City. This division only had a "little finishing to be done on the last two or three miles." Likewise, the work along the eastern division was now predicted to be completed the following year.[11]

As anticipated, some of the earliest settlers to Roscommon County utilized this road to access the area south of Houghton Lake. Also, lumbermen such as Thomas Nester would use this road to tote freight to their lumber camps in Roscommon County.

With the completion of this road, Roscommon County was "furnished with an outlet at all seasons of the year." It was predicted that during "the winter the immense amount of travel to and from the lumber camps along the route will make a stage route upon this road a paying institution, while the large number of land lookers, settlers and pleasure seekers who will visit Houghton Lake to bathe in its clear crystal waters and feast upon the fish that abound in it, will give to such a route an extensive patronage during the summer months."[12]

It is difficult to imagine the virgin forests that this road penetrated. What was it like to traverse this road prior to the great lumber harvest? We can join a correspondent for the *Midland Sun* who provided a rare account of a journey on this byway as part of a trip from Gladwin to Roscommon in 1884.

Leaving Meredith, the party proceeded north "through a hilly country covered with beautiful pine." This path would take them along the west boundary of Nester Township and eventually to Edna (Prudenville). The virgin forests were yet intact, and the trip's details provide an extraordinary view of a bygone forest. The correspondent observed that on "either side of the road as we sped along at a rate of eight miles per hour, are the most beautiful pines-mostly white, but occasionally a ridge of stately Norway; scarcely any other timber growing on these lands." This path brought them along the county line between Gladwin and Clare Counties proceeding north into Roscommon County. Entering Roscommon County, the State road did not follow today's M-18 but stayed due north along the Nester Township boundary.[13]

Following the township boundary, the travelers' view eventually changed, probably between sections 30 and 19 of West Nester Township. Here they "came to oak and jack pine openings" and several "valleys of a half mile, relieved by steep hills." Before leaving the township boundary they crossed "Field's railroad, a road some fourteen miles in length-of standard gauge-for logging purposes."[14]

Today with easy access to Roscommon County via Interstate 75, M-55 or US 27, it is hard to comprehend a time when the first mile of improved road into the county was a wagon road entering the county at the southwest corner of Nester Township. Equally difficult to absorb is that a trip "Up North" to Houghton Lake, that takes several hours today, was only possible by a sixty-mile journey on a wagon road from Midland, which would take more than a day.

CHAPTER 4

"The Greatest Project in Northern Michigan"

O f all the thousands of Irish families that immigrated to North America during the great diaspora of the late 1840s and early 1850s, the twelve-year-old son of one of these families would leave an indelible stamp on the development of the southeast corner of Roscommon County.

In 1846, like so many of his countrymen, Patrick Nester sought to escape the hard times and hunger brought on by the failure of the potato crop by securing passage to North America for his young family. They settled in Hamilton, Ontario, where Patrick found work practicing his Irish vocation, that of a blacksmith.

In 1851, at the age of 18, his son Thomas left for Michigan to follow the lumber trade. With drive, hard work and an eye to the future, his would be a true Horatio Alger story. First finding work in the winter of 1851–52 as an ox driver in Bay City, he moved in the spring to work at the Whitney sawmill in Bangor. Thomas relocated to Port Huron in 1852, finding employment originally at the Howard sawmill, then at A & H Fish. Over the next few years, he rose to head sawyer in the mill and would spend the winters in the logging camps, as chopper and teamster, earning a reputation as one of the best men on the drive.

His career could have stalled at this juncture if not for an oft-told event upon which pivoted his upward trajectory in the lumber

Thomas Nester (1833–1890)

industry. In 1855, Thomas, while working a night shift at the mill, observed that a raft of logs belonging to Avery & Murphy had become unsecured and was leaving the boom and entering the river. Soon 5,000,000 feet of logs, valued at $49,000 to $50,000, could have been dispersed downstream toward Lake St. Clair. Awakening Mr. Avery at his home, the "millionaire and the sawyer by their unaided exertion saved the raft, though not before Mr. Avery fell into the water. He would have been sucked under the logs and probably drowned had it not been for the promptitude of the young Irishman, who saved his life at the hazard of his own."[1]

Grateful for the actions of the intrepid sawyer, Mr. Avery, the next morning, persuaded Nester into his employ. For the following ten years, Nester worked a series of jobs for the firm, taking on the new responsibility of supervising small crews in the woods. Eventually, he was made superintendent of their sizable operations on the White River in Oceana County. His last three years with the firm were on the Pine River in Midland County.

Nester moved to Saginaw in 1862 and by 1865 was ready to go out on his own. He entered a partnership with W. L. Little and James F. Brown. Nester brought his experience into the woods, his partners brought mainly their capital. In three years, they each realized a $30,000 profit off of 1,500 acres. Nester next became affiliated with Jesse Hoyt, the co-founder of East Saginaw and a New York capitalist. They invested in Midland County pinelands and would, as in his previous arrangements, profit from Nester's operational skills. This partnership lasted until 1873 at which time Nester sold his interest to Hoyt.

Now with personal capital, Nester operated on his own, buying pinelands and harvesting the timber. With the Jackson, Lansing & Saginaw Railroad having been extended north through to Gaylord by 1873, new opportunities arose for sawmills to be located directly on this new line, penetrating the rich timber of the northern lower peninsula. Lumbermen were no longer constrained to having their mills at the mouths of major rivers and Nester joined the vanguard of lumbermen to take advantage of this. He constructed his mill at Wells Station in Arenac County. Though comfortably established at Wells and operating independently, Nester would soon reveal that he was amenable to new partners, especially if the size of the enterprise required it.[2] [3]

Pinelands that were relatively isolated from adequate waterways had previously been questionable investments when abundant timber was more favorably located. There was an economic limit to the distance a lumberman could haul logs in the winter. Lands beyond this limit languished until more accessible timber was harvested. By 1876, lumbermen in the North Country had started to embrace the use of logging railroads to provide the means of harvesting these relatively remote stands. Though railroad logging in Michigan dates back to the 1850s, their scale by the mid 1870s would change by an order of magnitude.[4]

As early as 1876, Nester began buying pinelands in southern Roscommon County, northern Gladwin County, and northeastern Clare County. Nester's interest in these purchases varied; some he owned exclusively, and in others he held a one-half or one-third interest. His partners also owned properties in which he held no interest. Besides his own logs and his partners, "he intended to put in a large quantity of other parties." As in the past, Nester would be the man on the ground.[5]

By the fall of 1877 Nester was initiating what the *Gladwin County Record* would report as "the greatest project in northern Michigan." The paper claimed that Nester was among "the first to profit by the successful experience of Gerrish & Hazelton" in the use of a logging railroad. His vision was to extend the reach of the Sugar River by building a railroad network into the hills of Gladwin, Roscommon, and eventually even Clare County.[6] [7]

Nester had been prompted to begin work by a recent fire through some of this timber. His initial railroad would be fifteen miles in length, "the longest of the kind commenced." Beginning at Lake Thomas (Atchel Lake on modern maps) in section 26, T. 21 N., R. 2 W., West Nester Township, the railroad would reach down the Sugar River into Gladwin County, traversing parts of T. 20 N., R. 2

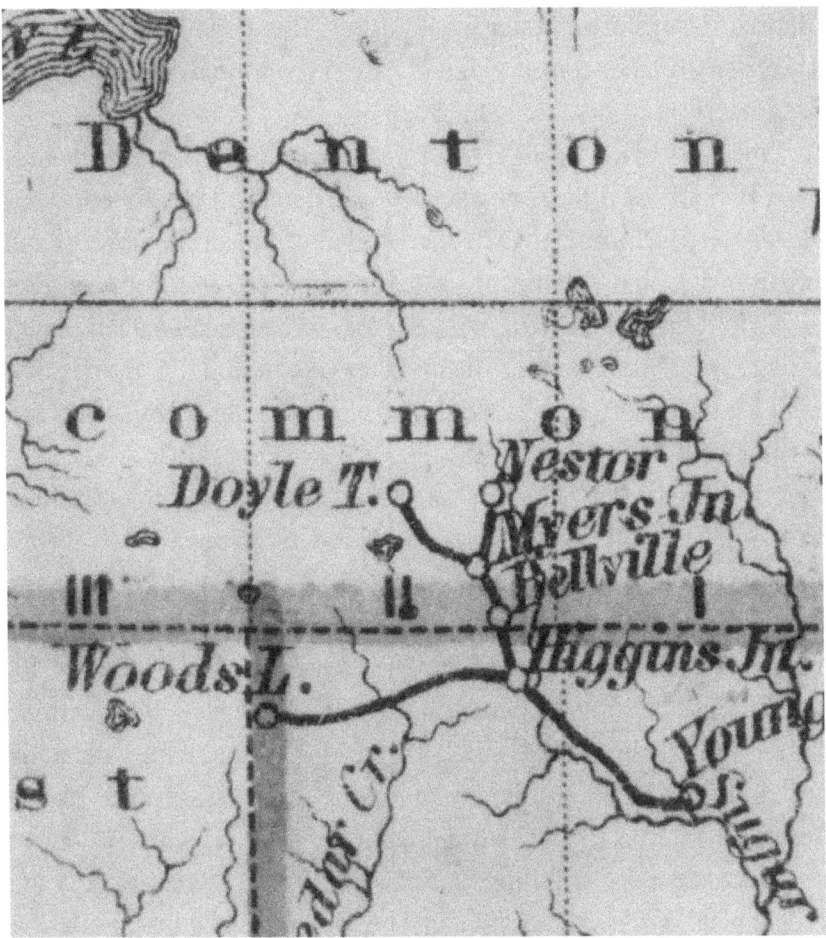

Map of Michigan. G. W. & C. B. Colton & Co. in the Office of the Librarian of Congress at Washington, 1878.

and 1 W., today's Sherman and Butman Townships. Nester had purchased much of the lands along the proposed route of the railroad. When unable to purchase the land outright, other arrangements were available. To continue his railroad south from Lake Thomas into Gladwin County, Nester planned on crossing section 2 in today's Sherman Township. To do this, he purchased a right of way for his railroad from Rust Eaton & Co. All through today's Sherman and

Butman Townships, Nester would follow this same plan. He would purchase the lands for his planned railroad route and, where needed, obtain a right of way for same.[8] [9] [10]

During April of 1878, Nester's operation was paid its first visit by staff of a local newspaper. This sojourn by the editor of *Roscommon Pioneer* provided a detailed report of the new village of Brundage on the shores of Lake Thomas. Here the editor reported seven buildings, some still in the process of construction. This small village would not retain the name Brundage for long. After this first visit by the newspaper, it would be referred to as Achill, Nester's birthplace in Ireland.

On the shore of his namesake lake, Thomas Nester placed his sawmill. The mill capacity was 30,000 board feet per day. It would provide the lumber for the framed buildings, sleighs, drays, bridges, dams, and railroad cars and ties. The mill machinery would also serve to hoist the logs out of the lake. The village had a 36' by 40' store in construction; a two-and-a-half-story, 40' by 110', barn with harness shop, hay storage and 84 horse stalls; a log barn with stalls for another 22 horses; a 26' by 40' framed repair shop with blacksmith facilities; a 26' by 70' framed boarding house; and a residence for the tradesmen, including Samuel T. Brundage, who oversaw the mechanical works of the village. The village boasted a population of 137.[11]

At the new boarding house, on the first Saturday of occupancy that month, the boys "celebrated the occasion with violin music, jig, clog, essence and other dancing and the amusements incident to camp life."[12]

The editor noted that the "roadbed is completed from the banks of the Sugar in section 20, T 20 N R1 W, in Gladwin County, to the sawmill at Lake Thomas. The ties are all out, the iron on the ground, and both being laid." It was reported that Nester had spent $20,000 and would be spending $12,000 more to have this first phase up and running.[13]

With no proximate rail connection, Nester, from the beginning, was forced to tote supplies in by wagon. Initially, it was reported in April of 1878 that the delivery of supplies would be expedited by cutting "a road through a four and one-half miles on the section line" from Lake Thomas intersecting "the Midland state road on the northwest corner of section 30" in T. 21 N., R. 2 W. Even if this road were ever built, it would be a long haul to the nearest railheads.[14]

To consummate this enterprise, what Nester truly needed was access to a railroad. To the south was the Flint & Pere Marquette Railroad. The small settlement of Cedar (later Gladwin) received freight and other services from Loomis, a station on the Flint & Pere Marquette Railroad, but Loomis was, straight-line from Achill, 28 miles away. Nester's solution was to construct his own road to Ogemaw Springs, a nascent settlement on the Michigan Central Railroad. The Michigan Central had leased this line from the Jackson, Lansing & Saginaw Railroad in August/September of 1871. Though the exact route of his road from Ogemaw Springs is lost to history, this pathway cut through the hills of Ogemaw and Roscommon Counties for about 20 miles. (The postal map on page 27 shows the delivery route for mail to Achill. Mail delivery could have logically followed Nester's road.) "Traversing an elevated country," his newly constructed road was "partly planked" and "in excellent condition" the entire year. Now supplies could be "hauled by wagons to Lake Thomas" from Ogemaw Springs.[15]

What impelled Nester to construct a new road from Ogemaw Springs? Isolated as Lake Thomas was, he must have believed that having his own direct route to a major railroad, capable of supplying him year-round, was essential. He also had another specific and daunting task: to bring in, from the outside world, the requisite heavy equipment to operate a freestanding railroad. Porter, Bell & Co. would supply Nester his initial locomotives, the first arriving in the spring of 1878. Incredibly, these "engines were taken over the rough road from Ogemaw station [Springs]."[16]

Besides the engines themselves, other ponderous materials needed to be brought to Lake Thomas. It was a herculean task, requiring substantial horsepower, to freight in steel rails over this distance. This was done repeatedly, as in March of 1880, when a correspondent, writing from Achill, noted that Nester had "been extremely busy for the past week, having over 20 teams engaged in hauling iron from Ogemaw for the purpose of extending his railroad."[17]

In June of 1878, the monumental activity in the northern part of Gladwin County garnered the attention of another local paper. The *Gladwin County Record* sent a writer to visit this great operation in the woods, though they noted that it "is not generally known by the citizens in this county what a prodigious lumbering enterprise is in progress in the northern part of the county."[18]

Some new facts were ascertained by the Gladwin writer during this trip. Foremost among these was a description of the dams being set in place on the Big Sugar. The first dam was reported as completed in the NW¼ of the NW¼ of section 20, township 20 north, range 1 west. Here the logs destined for Saginaw were being banked. Below this dam, a second was under construction in the SW¼ of NW¼ of section 21 in the same township as the upper dam. "The dams are constructed of sawed pine spiles, driven into the ground by a hammer weighing 2,300 lbs." The resulting 1,000 acres of water would provide the impetus to flush the logs down the Sugar River and into the Tittabawassee.[19]

The railroad, now referred to as the "Lake Thomas & Tittabawassee RR," was making eight trips a day from Lake Thomas south. One noteworthy bridge along the way was 800 feet long and 30 feet high. Aided by this rail system, one million board feet a week was being dumped into the Sugar River.[20]

With the sharp population increase in this corner of Roscommon County, it is not surprising that a new township was created in May of 1878. The new political township of Nester comprised both T. 21 N., R. 2 & 1 W. The township officials were the following:

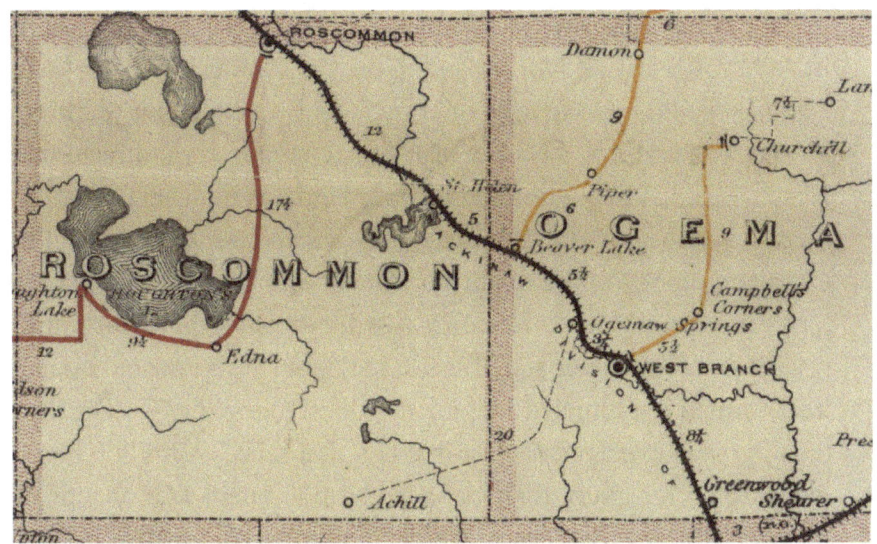

Post Route Map of the States of Michigan and Wisconsin, showing post offices, with intermediate distances between them and mail routes in operation on 1st April, 1884. Published by order of Postmaster General Walter Q. Gresham under the direction of C. Roeser Jr., topographer P.O. Dept., 1884.

supervisor, John Nester; clerk, John Mahon; treasurer, James Kelley; highway commissioner, Thomas Wagner; school inspector, John Nester; superintendent of schools, John Kelley.[21] [22]

Why would the mere establishment of a lumber camp compel the county to establish a new township? Truly, Brundage was more than a common lumber camp. Based on the simple number of buildings, Brundage rivaled Cedar (early name for the city of Gladwin), which claimed only eight buildings, three of which were residences, and it surpassed Houghton Lake, which housed only five resident families.[23] [24]

Seven months after this new township was established, on December 10, 1878, Nester's lumber operation triggered the establishment of the township's first post office. The first postmaster was Charles W. Meyers. Thomas Nester was surely instrumental in suggesting the name of this new post office. He had been born in Achill, County Mayo, Ireland. Now the lumber camp on Lake Thomas would no longer be referred to as Brundage, but Achill.[25]

As a testament to the sheer size and economic commitment that Nester was making, a third newspaper paid a visit during the summer; this time it was the trade paper, the *Lumberman's Gazette*. The *Gazette*'s report on the quality of timber and the size of Nester's harvest certainly gave an early justification for his substantial investment. The paper stated that a new branch line would open a tract "which is estimated will cut a million to the 'forty'. The logs thus far have averaged four or five to a thousand." A million board feet of pine for every forty acres and 1,000 board feet of lumber for every four or five logs was enviable timber. A seasonal harvest of between 12 and 15 million board feet was expected by fall. The paper also stated that Nester had about 8,000 acres to harvest containing an estimated 200,000,000 board feet.[26]

A hint of the size of the return on his investment that Nester was planning from this isolated tract of timber can be seen in one of his first sales of logs from September 1878. He sold 1,500,000 board feet for $12.00 per thousand and 1,000,000 board feet for $9.50 per thousand, for a total of $27,500.[27]

Thomas Nester was not one for self-promotion and the Saginaw papers struggled to glean any information from him about his new logging operation. When a writer for the *Saginaw Courier* "corralled" him in October of 1878, he was described as "one of the most wide awake and energetic, as well as enterprising lumbermen of Northern Michigan" but it was also noted that there were "few more reticent as to his own business affairs." Though reticent, Nester had reason to be proud of his operation and he talked about a few of his accomplishments and assets.[28]

He "was particularly happy over a most remarkable feat of log running accomplished by a force of men. On Wednesday, the 16th of October, the rear of a drive containing 5,000,000 feet was started from the terminus of his road on the Sugar," and on Sunday night "the drive was in the Tittabawassee boom at Saginaw, and the crew of fifteen men who did the work paid off and discharged Monday." Some of the logs were "in the tree" only the Monday before.[29]

In the interview, Nester demonstrated his awareness of the importance of heavy draft horses to move logs to rail side. He boasted that he had 25 span of horses that could not "be surpassed for excellence in the state." Eight more pairs were scheduled to be sent north for the coming winter.[30]

Lastly, unlike many of the major railroads in the state, Nester believed he had a railroad as clear of debt as any in Michigan, which he thought was "pretty good financiering for a 'green Irishman.'" Remarkably, Nester had brought this railroad to fruition without some of the local residents even knowing of its existence "until they heard the whistle of the locomotive." Their astonishment was warranted.[31]

By late fall of 1878, Nester had "a force of 150 men at work" and was "running four to six trains daily over his road" to the Sugar. He would need to keep this up for years to remove the estimated 600,000,000 board feet on the 20,000 acres subject to harvest via his railroad.[32]

Furthermore, that fall, Nester expanded his railroad network by beginning construction of a spur to the west toward today's Hoister Lake in North Gladwin County. This spur began on the main line just south of where it entered Gladwin County in section 2 and ran to the northeast corner of section 9 of T. 20 N., R. 2 W.

On this new spur, Charles Woods of Sanford would see to the harvest of 5,320 acres of pine "estimated at 100,000,000 feet and upwards." The acreage was located principally in northwestern Gladwin County, but also included parts of northeastern Clare County and southwestern Roscommon County. Woods planned on clearing a cedar swamp for log storage and building a dam to flood this denuded swamp. Lumbering was expected to begin the summer of 1879. It was "calculated to take ten years to complete the job."[33]

Only a year after first visiting Nester's operation, the *Lumbermen's Gazette* again sent a correspondent, in July 1879, to report on the noteworthy developments being undertaken in the hinterlands of Roscommon and Gladwin Counties.

What had transpired since the paper's last visit? Nester was rapidly expanding his rail network and the main line now proceeded northwest, past the line to Lake Thomas, to a small lake in section 28. Variously referred to as Conner's Lake, Nester Lake and Pine Lake, this lake would ultimately be referred to as Rollway Lake, an eponym taken from woods foreman John Mahon's sobriquet, "Rollway Jack." Mahon's headquarters would be located on the shores of this lake. Both Lake Thomas and Rollway Lake were used for log storage and Nester had installed "two parallel Ewert's detachable drive chains" for extracting the logs as high as 15 feet above the water to be loaded onto the railroad cars.[34] [35]

The new branch line being built for Charles Woods's operation was revealed to be the "most difficult part of the enterprise." This line had "a trestle work as substantially built as on a regular line of road, running over cuts 31 feet deep, and several fillings from 12 to 20 feet."[36]

Construction of the dam at the end of Charles Woods's branch had begun during the spring of 1879 and was completed by May of that year. George F. Keep of Midland oversaw building this enormous dam, which would span 300 feet. Like so much of what Nester did, the dam was "one of the largest in these parts." It was located between "sections 4 and 9, town 20, 2 west" and ultimately created Hoister Lake. The piles used to create the dam passed through 15 feet of muck and then were "driven from 4 to 6 feet into the clay and braced." The dam was reported to be "one of costliest and most durable in the country."[37] [38] [39]

Overall, for a logging railroad, this was construction eclipsing any in the state. As the *Gazette* drolly pointed out, Nester "did not find a roadbed already prepared in the wilderness, nor a level country, where he had only to lay his tracks upon the surface of the ground, with no other preparation than cutting the way through the trees. On the contrary, there were hills to cut through, streams to cross and morasses to pass." With the long term in mind, the track was laid "in a substantial manner, with culverts, embankments and bridges, as on an ordinary railroad." The main line was "ironed with 35 lb. and 40 lb. rails, and the branches and short line with 25 lb. rails."[40]

Two engines were in use, both manufactured by Porter, Bell & Co. The larger weighed 20 tons, and both had been hauled through the woods from Ogemaw Station. The number of logs being delivered down the railroad, in August, had reached astonishing levels. Twelve trains were being "run each way on the main line, 16 cars in each train." The cars carried "from 12 to 14 logs each, running four to six to the thousand feet." This is an average of nearly half a million board feet a day. Of course, this does not reflect the amount of lumber being cut a day. Logs were banked along the railroad and stored in the upper lakes until such times as capacity was available at the terminal lake and/or stream conditions allowed for driving them down the Sugar River.[41]

How was it that Nester had the expertise to construct such a railroad? The "bridges, etc., were erected by a man of great experience in such matters." Though the identity of this man was not noted, Nester was blessed by the fact that his brother John, who was in his employ, had completed contracts for the construction of 25 miles of the Michigan Central Railroad north of Grayling.[42] [43]

The terminus of the railroad was located at the artificial lake engineered by Nester. As mentioned, this lake was created by damming the Sugar River. The dam was made by "sheet-piling the entire distance of sawed timber driven tight together, the joints caulked with oakum." At this lake, the track ran "over the water for a quarter of a mile on a substantial trestle." At the side of the trestle was a "dock ten feet wide and extending the length of the train." From the dock ran a "series of skids" to carry the logs to the water.[44]

"Taken altogether this is an enterprise of no small magnitude," extolled the *Gazette*. Nester had invested "upwards of $100,000" in a project that was exclaimed to be "a fair exemplification of the pluck and energy of the men engaged in the lumber trade of Michigan, of whom Mr. Nester" it was believed, was "not one of the least."[45]

Seemingly, Nester would have had his hands full commanding such a sprawling lumber operation to the extent that he would not be eager to take on additional projects. However, in late 1878, he took a contract to build a road from Wells Station west to the Gladwin County line. Wells Station was on the Michigan Central Railroad in northern Bay County (today's Arenac County). This new road that Nester built would enter Gladwin County in section 25, T. 20 N., R. 2 E. He would extend the road farther west, and by December of 1878, he had "the road from the dam on the Big Sugar to Wells station half completed." By February, having just completed this project, "he drove over the new road from Wells to Lake Thomas." Now supplies could be hauled from his mill at Wells Station to the terminus of his railroad in Gladwin County.[46] [47] [48] [49]

Astonished by the breadth of Nester's developments, the *Saginawian* facetiously claimed that the "state can go out of the road making business soon, for Tom Nester in getting around to his several camps will have either railroads or logging roads built throughout the entire lower peninsula."[50]

CHAPTER 5

Mr. Nester's Army

I t was, in many ways, an army with a military-like presence that had invaded West Nester Township. It was not there to confront a human enemy, but an ancient forest that had grown there since the glacial retreat over 10,000 years ago. Like most armies of the day, Nester's was almost exclusively comprised of men in their twenties and thirties. These troops (shanty boys) were deployed over the southern half of West Nester Township in what seems to be four camps, based on the snapshot taken in early June by the Federal Census of 1880.[1]

Unique for this time and place, the 1880 census for Nester Township reports there solely the lumbering operation of Thomas Nester. It is a roll call of 230 men, 4 wives and two daughters. At this time, there were no other lumber camps or settlers recorded in the township.

The census documented only living quarters, without the ancillary buildings typical of a lumber camp. The headquarters, at Achill, housed the only women and families. There were four buildings that housed these families. They were occupied by the following: William Conners, the log scaler with wife and daughter; Uriah Chester, the carpenter with wife and daughter; Wesley Dulmage, a

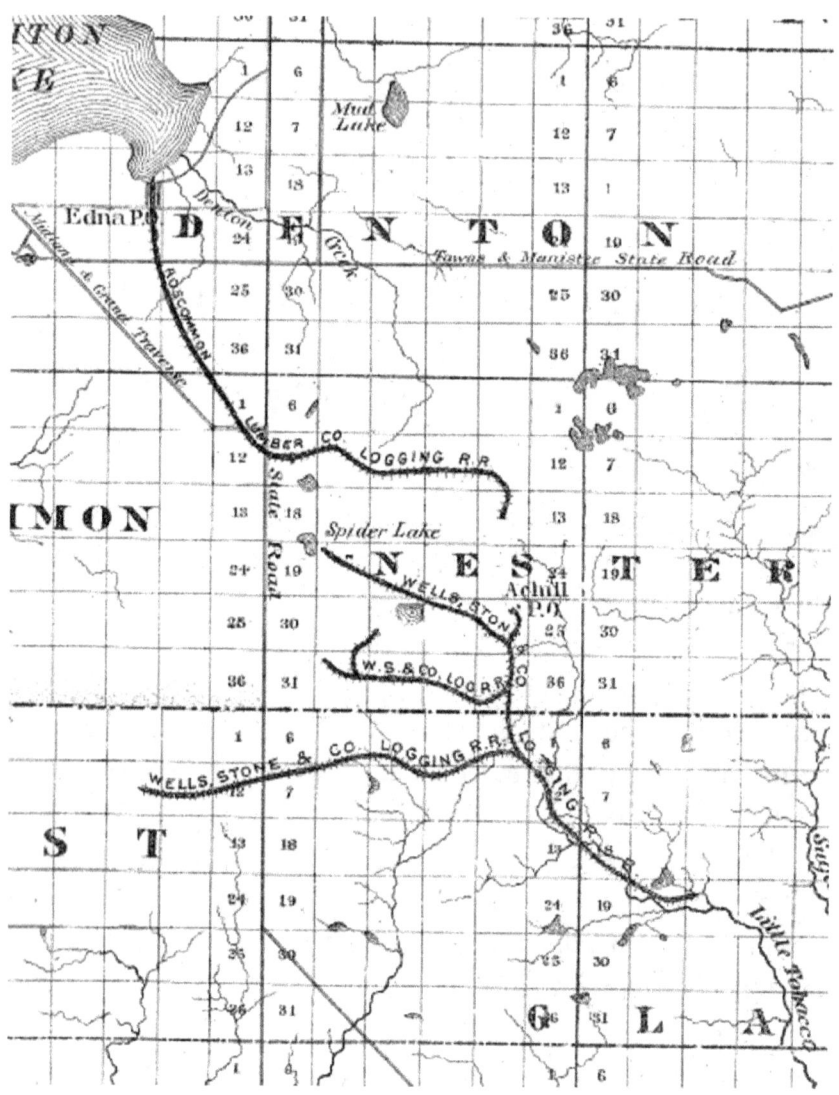

Tackabury's Atlas of the State of Michigan, Walling,
Henry Francis, G.N. Tackabury, Detroit, 1884.

Note that for this map the two railroads are shown unconnected. The
Sugar River is misidentified as the Little Tobacco.

woods foreman with wife; and William Munderback, a woods cook with wife.

Four other dwellings were noted in the census. Based on the dates and order of visitation, each of these other dwellings would appear to be an individual camp, though one was probably at Achill.

One camp was run by John Mahon, woods foreman and Thomas Nester's brother-in-law. Thirty-six men were employed here. All were listed as laborers except one woods cook. The second camp held 32 men, headed by Samuel Smith. The third camp, overseen by John Higgins, sheltered 48 shanty boys including two cooks, a carpenter, and a difficult-to-explain bartender. Perhaps he was only a visitor. James Kelly, train foreman, ran the last and largest camp, which was comprised of 108 men. His personnel included a woods cook, machinist, blacksmith, carpenter, shingle weaver, and store clerk. This was likely Achill given that the company store was in this camp.

Unlike most logging efforts of the day, Nester's operation was conducted essentially year-round. This was not the seasonal work in the woods typical of lumber camps not afforded the benefits of a railroad. Those outfits relied on winter weather to move logs. Nester had no compunction about utilizing the new technology (logging railroads) to the fullest. The census reflects this year-round employment. Most of the men indicated that they had been unemployed only a few months out of the year, if at all.

Who made up this army? As mentioned, it was primarily young men. Of the few men over forty (12 individuals), five of them held specialty jobs such as woods cook, machinist, carpenter, and blacksmith. These occupations kept them insulated from the more operose jobs in the woods.

The ranks of this army were mostly foreign born. Over half (131) hailed from Canada and 26 from Ireland. Only 28 were born Wolverines. Twenty came from the Empire State, New York. The remainder of the US-born were from such states as Pennsylvania, Wisconsin, Ohio, New Hampshire, Maine, Maryland, and Massachusetts. Other foreign-born laborers were from Scotland, Holland, and England. All were white except three native North Americans from New Brunswick.

CHAPTER 6

Nester Settles In

N ester and his partners had obviously been investing for the long term. The isolation and size of their timber holdings demanded this. Small timber parcels along a navigable stream required relatively little investment to harvest the timber and bring that timber to a riverbank. But that was a world apart from what was being accomplished by this partnership. Everything here was on a grand scale and demanded money, time, and long-term planning.

Besides the complex network of railroads, dam building, and stream clearing, Nester and his partners would also develop a large agricultural complex, utilizing hundreds of acres to supply fresh food for his men as well as pasturage and shelter for his horses and other farm animals.

To this end, Thomas Nester had purchased approximately two sections of land near the junction of the Little Sugar River and the Big Sugar River. Most of the acreage was in section 3, T. 19 N., R. 1 W. and section 34, T. 20 N., R. 1 W. In section 3, during August of 1879, "William Young with a crew of 12 men, went into the forest and commenced clearing land, and at the end of October they had 250 acres of hardwood land chopped and cleared, ready for the plow." Within a year, 300 acres were ready for the plow. Over 200 of these acres had been planted during the spring of 1880, largely with oats and millet. Lesser acreage of potatoes, turnips, carrots, and peas were also cultivated this first year. Additionally, a large orchard of fruit trees had been set out.[1] [2]

There were "employed on the farm from 20 to 30 men and seven working teams, engaged in logging and plowing, getting in crops, etc." during the summer of 1880. The men did double duty for Nester and were "employed two days in the week in driving the logs out of the Sugar put in by the railroad."[3]

The buildings for the farm were located in the northeast corner of section 3. Late in 1879, Nester began construction of one of the first buildings on his "new" farm. This was a 30' x 40' house. It would, by 1881, have a 20' x 20' addition. Additionally located on the farm was a "root-house 24 X 30, 10 feet high, on the inside" and a "respectable barn 40 X 60." There were also a "blacksmith shop and sleeping camps for the men." As a testament to the celerity in which wilderness could be converted to agriculture, alongside these buildings on the Little Sugar was "the hut of a pioneer trapper, which a few years ago was the only building that graced the spot."[4] [5]

Besides the typical structures expected on a farm, there was one particularly newsworthy building. This remarkable building was of such colossal size that the Gladwin paper would not only claim "it to be without doubt the largest barn in the state," but in 1882 it would state that it "is probably the largest frame barn in the world." This unparalleled edifice was built on Nester's main farm in section three on the banks of the Little Sugar River just upstream from its confluence with the Big Sugar River.[6] [7]

By the summer of 1880, Nester had plans for this enormous barn, but it was not until May of 1881 that reports of its actual inception appear in the local paper. In August 1881 during a visit to Nester's operation, the editor of the *Gladwin County Record* described the barn: the "main part of the barn is 106 feet long; there is a wing on the west side 80 feet long, both being 50 feet wide. The structure is three stories high with 16 feet posts to each story, and is 75 feet in height from base to apex of roof. It is estimated that 500,000 feet of lumber and 80,000 shingles will be used in its construction, also 156 main posts 16-feet long and 800 braces. The first story will be used for stables, root-houses, etc., the second for hay and the third for grain. The first two stories of the barn are built under a bank on the Little Sugar, so that a driveway leads from the bank through the third floor of the building. The driveway is 16 feet wide, and the bank being V-shaped, a wagon may be driven into the wing or main building and out at the opposite side. A driveway will also lead into the wing on the second floor. It is estimated that the barn will contain 720 tons of hay under the beams. Upwards of 100 tons are now stored in one [of] the mows, and scarcely fill one corner. The lumber and shingles in the barn were sawed at Mr. Nester's mill at Achill. At the usual prices for lumber and work, it will readily be seen that this barn will stand Mr. Nester in $10,000."[8] [9] [10]

To the north, in section 34, T. 20 N., R. 1 W., ground was also being cleared. Here a crew under James Doyle had 40 acres ready for cultivation by the summer of 1881. To the west of this farm, in section 33, was the Stone, Nester & Co. farm. Seventeen men and ten teams of horses were adding to the 100 acres already cleared in this section. By the summer of 1881, buildings on the Stone, Nester & Co. farm included a 24' x 36' house and a 36' x 70' barn.[11]

Besides developing his farms, Nester was also expanding his railroad network. In the spring of 1880, an extension was being laid from "the southeast quarter of section 28, town 21, 2 west, to a small lake on section 18, same town, a distance of about four miles." This small lake in section 18 is today's Doyle Lake, most likely named after Nester's woods foreman, James Doyle.[12]

• • • • •

Once pinelands were harvested, they were particularly susceptible to fires given the huge amount of fuel left on the ground. And like any settlement so located in Northern Michigan, Achill itself was extremely vulnerable to fires given both the building materials and its location in a rapidly growing expanse of pine slash. Whether by building fires or forest fires, the danger was substantial.

On Monday night, February 16, 1880, a fire caused serious damage to a building at Achill. The building was "used as an office, etc., and was nicely furnished, being carpeted and fitted up for the use of employers and overseers." Originating near a stovepipe, the fire caused about $2,000 of damage. Less than a year later, on Tuesday morning, January 4, 1881, another building fire ravaged the blacksmith shop and store at Achill.[13][14]

The real threat to a sprawling lumbering operation, such as Nester's, however, was a forest fire, and to assess how common forest fires were, it is as simple as noting the ubiquitous charred pine stumps from that era that cover so many of the northern townships. West Nester was no exception.

On Saturday, June 11, 1881, the village of Achill was threatened by raging flames. "Nester's whole force of men" fought the fire. The men were successful in saving the sawmill and store, but "Nester sustained considerable damage on his railroad stock, as some cars were burned and quite an amount of track injured by the fire heating the iron." The fires had run wild all week and other camps were at risk. At Charles Woods's camp on the Cedar, 8,000,000 feet of stacked logs were saved by "the foreman, John McFarlin, and his full force of men." But on the open acreage cut the previous season, nothing was left but "the black ground, and occasionally a black stump." Fortuitously, it was believed that little damage was done to the standing timber.[15]

• • • • •

Nester and his partners' annual harvest would grow from about 23 million board feet for the 1878–79 season to almost double that in the 1879–80 season. A report from January of 1880 illustrates what a daily harvest during the winter involved to achieve these numbers. Nester was "putting in upwards of 300,000 feet of logs a day." Additionally, Stone, Nester & Co. was putting in about 75,000 feet per day while Charles Woods was harvesting 80–90,000 feet per day. Some of the logs would proceed to the Sugar River while the remainder would be stored in the various ponds and lakes.[16] [17] [18]

Some idea of what a day's work was like, to achieve such harvest figures, comes from William Young during February of 1880. He reported that at his camp "800 logs were put in that scaled 150,000 feet, with four teams on a ¾- mile haul, in twelve hours." Proud of his crew, Young challenged any Gladwin crew to "beat this and do as much the next day."[19]

One means to achieve a record day's work like this was to increase the board feet of logs on each sleigh load. Crews took excessive pride in the size of the loads they hauled. Bragging loads were often reported or photographed. On Saturday, November 27, 1880, a "load of logs scaling 9,240 feet was hauled at Chas. Woods' camps." "The load was hauled on [a] pole road by one team, 1-1/2 miles, Wm. Hibbard teamster." The next season, at a Stone, Nester & Co. camp, "one team hauled one load containing ten logs that scaled 7,360 feet."[20] [21]

This timber was worthy of Nester's efforts. During another visit by the staff of the *Gladwin County Record* in the spring of 1880, it was reported that at Wood's Pond they were hauling "logs that aver-age 4-1/2 to the thousand feet." These were 16-foot logs averaging over 220 board feet per log and 19" in diameter. Stump diameter would be noticeably higher than this 19" average, illustrating the size of the trees being harvested.[22]

Another gauge of the exceptional timber found on the partners' forestlands comes from reports of the occasional individual tree of remarkable stature. Two reported giants were brought to the attention of the *Gladwin County Record* during a visit to the paper office by Charles Woods. These trees "scaled respectively over 6,000 and 8,000 feet each." They were claimed to be "the two largest trees ever cut in the state."[23]

At Wood's Pond or Hoister Lake, the hoister bridge was "1,100 feet in length and 46 feet high." The steam-powered and mechanized work being done there was later described by the same paper in July of 1880: "About 200 [feet] from the end of this bridge is attached the hoisting apparatus, by means of which logs are taken from the lake and hoisted upon the bridge, by steam power at the rate of 10 logs per minute, two endless chains running over pullies being attached on a slide, on this chain at equal distances apart are fastened the hoisting arrangemant *[sic]*, which consists of an iron jaw. One man on the lake rolls the log up against the slide, and as the chain brings the hoister around, two or more logs are taken up the slide. When as they drop on the skids they are scaled, and two cant hook men roll them on the skidway to the cars. It takes about an hour to load the train, and an hour to make the trip to the landing and return."[24]

As the country between Woods's operation and Lake Thomas was traversed, the reporters encountered pine "tracts estimated to contain 1,500,000 feet to the forty acres." Not only were these stands of mature timber, as noted by the size of the logs, the region must also have been densely covered with pine trees in order to contain this staggering amount of board feet per forty acres.[25]

To get these logs to the Sugar River, at times, the railroad would run 24 hours a day. In September 1880, ten trips were "made over the road and 350,000 feet of logs put into the Sugar every 24 hours." The schedule had not changed much a year later when trains were "running on the Nester railway night and day, making 12 trips every 24 hours." That September (1881) they were taking logs out of Rollway Lake in section 28. The amount of board feet reported being put into the Sugar per day in September was nearly identical each year, between 350,000 and 400,000 board feet.[26] [27]

After the logs were delivered to the dam ponds, they were eventually made ready to be driven down stream en masse. Log drives on the Sugar took place after the spring thaw, when adequate water was available to flush logs downstream and when space was available in the Tittabawassee.

On Monday, July 19, 1880, "Nester's folks cleaned the Sugar of 9,000,000 feet of logs at one sweep." "The dams on the Sugar were opened, and the logs in the Tittabawassee were jammed together, clearing a space of seven miles. Upon starting the logs in the Sugar, they were all taken out by force of water." Despite this drive, Nester struggled getting his logs downstream, perhaps because of the river being full of logs or lack of water later in the season. Determined to see improvement in 1881, he swore "by the 'great horn spoons' that his logs" were coming down in 1881. By late 1881 it could be claimed by Nester's crews that "logs when banked are only ten hours' run to the Tittabawassee dam."[28] [29] [30]

William Young had "charge of the driving operations on the Sugar." He earned a well-deserved reputation for these skills as he was a versatile and valuable employee of Nester's. He was also the "genial foreman of the farm," while in the winter he was one of Nester's woods foremen. Young Lake in section 17, near one of Nester's camps, is believed to be named after him. Typically impressed by Young's driving skills, the *Gladwin County Record* afforded him this compliment, that one has got "to get up in the morning when you get ahead of Billy Young driving logs."[31] [32] [33]

How did all of this relate to the partner's pecuniary interests? In the spring of 1880, the season's pricing for logs delivered to Saginaw was expected to "range from $10 to $14 per thousand" board feet. In May, David Ward sold "1,000,000 feet of cork pine logs at $15.75 per m feet, (one thousand board feet), said to be the highest price ever paid for pine saw logs in this state." Though pricing varied throughout the year, Nester and his partners undoubtedly received pricing in this range. Even at $12 per thousand board feet average, every 10 million board feet brought in a small fortune at $120,000.[34] [35]

This of course was not pure profit. Wages had to be paid. A summary of the wage situation for 1881 stated that "wages paid in the woods are from $1 to $2 higher, a month, than last year. Common laborers are receiving from $22 to $26 a month. Men having positions of more or less responsibility are being paid a slight advance over that of last year's wages. Men are very plenty, and no further advance is anticipated."[36]

Nester had approximately 230 men working for him, based on census information for Nester Township, but he also had men employed at Woods's camp, at the dams and the farms, all in Gladwin County. Simply looking at the crew in Nester Township and a $25-per-month year-round wage, annual labor costs would have been around $69,000, though certainly not all of these men would have been employed year-round.

• • • • •

It could easily be construed that the area in which Nester operated was one contiguous piece of property under single ownership. Yet, on the contrary, a jumbled patchwork of ownership existed. Nester owned thousands of acres outright as well as having one-half or one-third ownership of thousands of other acres. His partners also owned lands in which Nester held no interest. Their lands were scattered over six surveyed townships, all riddled with inholdings.

Among noteworthy inholdings were those of Rust, Eaton & Company. Nester had a contract to transport this firm's logs down the Woods's branch of his railroad. Rust, Eaton & Company owned a large tract of pineland on the Roscommon/Gladwin boundary near this branch of the railroad. Rust Eaton Lake along this border was named after the firm.[37] [38]

Unlike Rust, Eaton & Co. who contracted with Nester to have their logs transported down Nester's railroad but harvested their own timber, Ryan, Johnson & Co. of Detroit arranged to have Nester do all of the work for three-eighths of the value of the logs delivered to the boom limits. This company owned 320 acres of timber in sections 1 and 10 of T. 20 N., R. 2 W.[39]

Undoubtedly, over time, many other such arrangements were contracted with Nester for he had one undeniable monopolistic resource: his railroad. This railroad was the only economic avenue to move logs out of this region without an impractical long haul.

· · · · ·

From the beginning of the township in 1878, through 1881, Nester employees dominated township offices. Though this could be seen as undue influence on an electorate, the only citizens living in the township were Nester employees. Tom Nester's brother, John, served as the original township supervisor. By 1880, William M. Conners, log scaler for Thomas Nester, was the supervisor. William Minnis, Nester's bookkeeper took over the position in 1881 after the resignation of Uriah Chester, Nester's "master mechanic, for the construction of bridges, cars, buildings etc."[40] [41]

· · · · ·

By the end of 1881, Nester's railroad network had reached well beyond the early route from Lake Thomas to the Sugar River. To the northwest, it extended to Rollway Lake and beyond, splitting into two branches, one to Doyle Lake and another to Young Lake. As mentioned, in Gladwin County, Charles Woods's Branch left the main line and extended east past the Cedar River. Though steel rails would regularly be brought into the forest to expand the network, Nester's foremen did not hesitate to utilize temporary pole roads where needed. Pole roads as described in Michigan in 1883, "had poles laid down and pinned to the ground" where "horses draw cars having wheels made concave to fit the poles."[42]

At both Woods's and Rollway Jack's camps, pole roads were used during the spring of 1880. These temporary pathways met the immediate demand to move logs during snow-free months without laying steel rails. Sixty to seventy thousand board feet of logs were "being put in daily on pole road" into Wood's Pond in April of 1880. Likewise, at Pine (Rollway) Lake visitors found "Rollway Jack with his crew, rushing logs into the lake by means of a pole road" three months later.[43] [44]

CHAPTER 7

The Big Sale

I t would seem inconceivable, given his large investment, great success and keen involvement overseeing such an expansive operation, that Thomas Nester would be looking beyond his enterprise in Roscommon and Gladwin Counties, but indeed he was. Lumbermen, of this era, by the very nature of their industry, had to constantly purchase timberlands as a means of sustaining their involvement in the business. It was an extractive process. There was no consideration for sustained yields or of select cutting. For any given parcel, this was a onetime event, harvesting the wealth from an ancient forest.

With the help of his brother, Tim, it soon became clear where Nester was looking to the future: the relatively untouched Upper Peninsula of Michigan. In April of 1880, Tim Nester proceeded to the city of Ontonagon, "where he purchased for his brother what would now sell for millions of dollars." The increase in value claimed here is notable as it was reported only three years after Nester's original purchase of the land. Nester had acquired "a tract of pine known as the Ward lands, containing about 9,000 acres, consideration about $75,000." This tract was "said to be the most valuable on the market" the lands being "on the main Ontonagon river and the south fork of the west branch of the Ontonagon river." Nester would continue to purchase lands in the western Upper Peninsula and even invest in the Ontonagon & Brule River Railroad.[1] [2]

With his eye focused on the Upper Peninsula, Nester needed to disengage from his partners.

One of the first indications that Nester was seriously looking to sell his interest in the operation was reported in March of 1881. "We learn that T. H. McGraw & Co. have the refusal for 90 days of the purchase of Thos. Nester's interest in the northern part of this county," announced the *Gladwin County Record*. Though nothing materialized between Nester and McGraw, Nester was obviously showing his hand to his partners. He wanted out. He even started selling his Wells station lands by September of 1881, selling 360 acres to his brother-in-law, P. A. O'Donnell.[3] [4]

To speculate about the machinations between Nester and his partners is fruitless, but some arm wrestling was occurring. Whereas in the spring, Nester was courting a buyer, now, in November, his partners allegedly had found one of their own. The reports stated that a "large land sale took place on Saturday, by which Sibley & Bearinger become owners of all the interest of A. W. Wright, C. W. Wells, and C. F. Stone in the firm of Stone, Nester & Co., and of the firm Thomas Nester & Co., subject to Thomas Nester's right to buy the same within ten days." Furthermore, the report indicated that, "Thos Nester intends to take the lands, and offers them for sale, together with his railroad, lumber equipage, and 70,000,000 feet standing timber besides."[5]

If Nester could secure a buyer or buyers for both his partners' interests and his own, he could utilize his right within the ten days to match the offer from Sibley & Bearinger.

Besides the acreage and pine, Nester listed what else would be included in the sale as follows: "There is upon the property a first class railroad, about 17 miles now in operation, with three branches, running through the heart of the pine, two locomotives, engine and machinery for hoisting logs from the lakes, and all necessary and modern equipments, good dam and banking grounds, and logs when banked are only ten hours' run to the Tittabawassee dam; also one circular saw mill for cutting timber and ties for the railroad; two farms of about 1,800 acres with first-class dwellings and barns thereon, about 650 acres cleared and under cultivation; 20 pairs of good horses and harnesses, about 40 to 50 sets of good log sleighs, 8 to 12 sets of pole cars, camp equipage for about five camps, 10 or 12 wagons and trucks, frame store and storehouses, about 150 tons of hay, about 1,100 bushels of potatoes, about 1,500 bushels of bagas, and all supplies on hand at a fair price."[6]

His partners' interest was over 11,840 acres, some of which Nester owned a one-third or one-half interest. He owned outright 12,080 acres. The amount of pine on the combined lands was estimated at 320 million board feet, 250 on the partners' lands and 70 on Nester's.[7]

Nester offered these properties until "Wednesday, November 23rd, 1881, at noon, in separate parcels or all in one body to suit purchaser." He warned off specious inquiries stating: "I do not desire to banter, but am ready to talk business to all who may be interested."[8]

The *Saginaw Herald* even reported on Saturday, November 26, 1881, that the papers were signed, sealed, and delivered, just the night before, on a great land sale. Sibley & Bearinger had bought all the interest of Wells, Stone & Company in Thomas Nester & Company's pine lands, teams, etc.

Though claims of sales to other parties were reported in the papers, none of them came to fruition. It was all a dance to garner better positioning to negotiate. Deadlines expired, deals failed to materialize, and partners just stared each other down. It was all posturing.

Nester, though, held an ace up his sleeve. He owned the locomotives and rolling stock. He owned, outright, most of the lands on which the railroad and dams lay. This was the conduit to the Sugar River, hence the avenue to Saginaw. A new party may have been cautious to buy out Nester's partners' interests, given the control Nester held in the only economical route to remove timber. At least these facts may have softened the price being asked by his partners.

The first sign that a deal had been completed was a report of some unusual behavior on the part of certain staid citizens of Saginaw. During the last week of December, "Thomas Nester, John Brown and John Rust were among those assessed for fast driving on the streets of Saginaw." Unusual, indeed. What was not yet fully public was that on Tuesday of that week, Nester had sold all his interest in the soon to be referred to "Nester Tract."[9]

The *Saginaw Herald* of Sunday, January 1, 1882, announced to the public the deal that had been signed five days prior, stating "Nester Pine Lands Sold – Wells, Stone & Co. the Purchasers – Consideration $510,000." Nester was out, free to pursue a new chapter in his lumbering career in the Upper Peninsula.[10]

Included in the sale of the land was "also the Railroad heretofore operated by Nester from the dam on Sec 21 T. 20 N, R 1W to a point on Sec 18, T 21 N R2 W with its two branches as now located on any of above lands with the road bed superstructure and rails of Said road across above lands with the buildings, improvements and constructions thereon and the engines cars and rolling stock of every description as well as the tools materials and implements pro-cured for and used upon said rail road for the sum of three hundred thousand dollars."[11]

The several firms in which Nester and his partners were involved also had millions of board feet of logs and sawn timber in process yet to be sold. Included were five "millions sawed lumber on the river, 31,000,000 of logs in the Tittabawassee boom and 16,000,000 of marked logs on the banking grounds or afloat in the streams."[12]

In the articles of agreement between Thomas Nester and Ammi Wright et al, the deal was valued at $450,000 less monies owed for

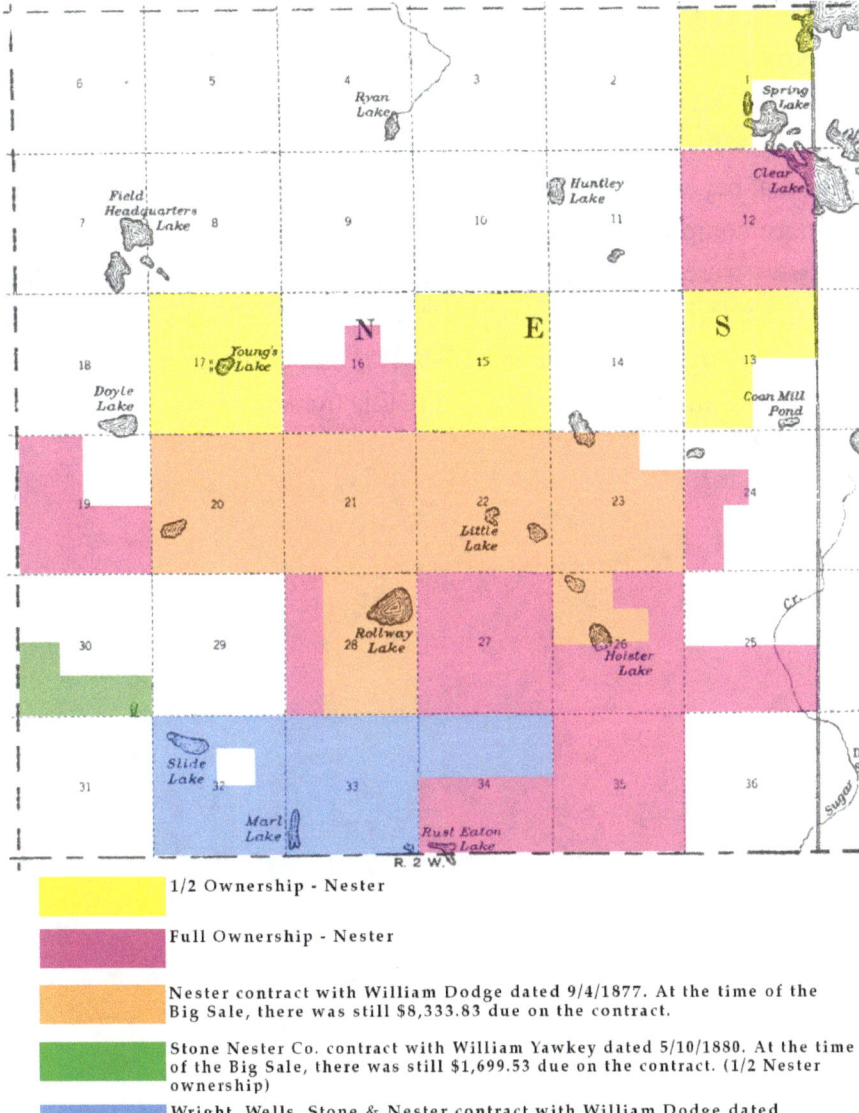

1/2 Ownership - Nester

Full Ownership - Nester

Nester contract with William Dodge dated 9/4/1877. At the time of the Big Sale, there was still $8,333.83 due on the contract.

Stone Nester Co. contract with William Yawkey dated 5/10/1880. At the time of the Big Sale, there was still $1,699.53 due on the contract. (1/2 Nester ownership)

Wright, Wells, Stone & Nester contract with William Dodge dated 8/28/1878. At the time of the Big Sale, there was still $53,571.44 due on the contract. (1/3 Nester ownership)

Above are the lands in West Nester Township involved in the "Big Sale" of December 27, 1881. The Yawkey contract also included approximately 40 acres in Roscommon Township. The Dodge contract of 8/28/1878 also included approximately 5,213.5 acres in Sherman Township, Gladwin County, Roscommon Township, Roscommon County, and Franklin Township, Clare County.

some outstanding purchase agreements for land on Nester's part and money allotted for a recent camp that Nester had built, as well as some wages for that camp on Wright and his partners' part.[13]

It is difficult to reconcile these figures. All that can be assumed is that beyond the recorded deed (12/27/1881 for $300,000) and the more comprehensive agreement (12/31/1881 for $450,000) other assets were involved by the time the $510,000 was reported in the papers during early January of 1882.

The *Saginaw Herald* would call it "one of the largest, if not the largest transaction ever handled in this market."[14]

CHAPTER 8

Wright, Wells, and Stone Take Over

T he great lumber harvest on the "Nester" tract would continue unabated, but without Thomas Nester. His partners, Ammi Wright, Charles Wells, and Farnum Stone would now direct the enterprise. By July of 1882, the partners realized that consolidating their various companies, all having mixed ownership, would be in their best interest. With that in mind, a pool was "effected of the timber, lumber and mill operations of A. W. Wright & Co., Wright & Knowlton, and Wells, Stone & Co. of Saginaw City whereby the sawmill, planing mill and lumber yard located there, and 350,000,000 feet of pine timber" would all be consolidated by January 1, 1883. The stockholders were "Ami *[sic]* W. Wright of Saratoga, Charles W. Wells, F. C. Stone, Willis F. Knowlton and Wm. H. Wright of Saginaw City and Oscar D. Wetherell of Chicago." Sixty thousand shares were issued at $25 a share.[1][2]

Though the absence of Thomas Nester was significant, much would continue as before with many of the same employees in place and production holding at similar levels. In April of 1882, the company was "putting in 200,000 feet daily" into the Sugar River with logs being "driven out every other day." By late June, Charles Woods had completed his cut for the year on the north branch of the Cedar having put in 9,000,000 feet. All his logs had been drawn up from Wood's Pond and carried by rail to the Sugar. The rail men then focused on emptying Rollway Lake of timber. Here in early July the report was "eight trains daily, drawing 16 cars to a trip, each train 35,000 to 40,000 feet."[3][4][5]

As ever, fire was a constant danger. Later that July, carelessness led to a fire on Rollway Lake. The fire "burned some logs, the hoister and keeled the engine into the lake." Undeterred by this setback, the company was erecting two new buildings at Achill, both 30' x 50', and adding a 2.5-mile-long branch railroad.[6]

In December of 1882, the editor of the *Ogemaw Herald* toured, by sleigh, the soon to be consolidated A.W. Wright Lumber Company's expansive enterprise. At the headquarters camp (Achill) they met with Superintendent West Dulmage and bookkeeper Charles Myers. First on their itinerary was a visit to the camps that the *Herald* stated were "by far the best appointed and operated of any in this part of the state." There were "four camps of about 70 men each respectively under the charge of the following foremen: No. 1, A. Scholfield, No. 2, A. Young, No. 3, A.V. Cribbey, No. 4, John J. Young." The men were "busily at work getting into the Sugar River some 40,000,000 [feet] of as fine timber as was ever cut in Michigan."[7]

The editor was particularly impressed with the large agricultural operation that supported the lumber harvest. Of the 600 acres that had been under cultivation the past year, the following harvest was tallied: "wheat 500 bushels; oats 4,000 bushels; hay 250 tons; potatoes 1,900 bushels; cabbage 5,500; pickles 19 barrels; turnips 3,000 bushels; onions 300 bushels; beets 200 bushels; and all other things usually grown on a farm in proportions."[8]

In early 1883 the most significant development to affect West Nester since its namesake's arrival was already being revealed. The

Harrison Cleaver on January 4, 1883, reported that "Samuel Cary, the F. & P. M. company's surveyor, arrived in town on Monday last and is now working northeast from the end of the iron with the survey. Operations are to begin at once and twelve miles of the road is to be built as soon as possible. We understand it is to be connected with the Wells, Stone & Co.'s road north east of here, known as the Nester road."[9]

Things were changing indeed. No longer would supplies have to be toted in from Ogemaw Station or up the Midland, Houghton Lake & Traverse Bay State Road from Midland or from Wells Station. However, prior to this new avenue being available to the township, the Wright Lumber Company had some work of its own to do.

For the Wright Lumber Company to utilize the coming Harrison branch of the Flint & Pere Marquette Railroad that would terminate at the yet unfounded village of Meredith, the company would need to build a line from the dam west toward this future village. By July of 1883, the company had already begun work on a new branch that would leave the Lake Thomas railroad where it crossed the township boundary between townships T. 20 N., R. 2 & 1 W. From this intersection, the new railroad was built almost directly west to the future terminus of the Harrison Branch. By October of 1883, the rail lines were connected, finally bringing a direct rail link to the outside world (map, p. 56). Today, four miles of this line can be driven by car east out of Meredith.[10] [11]

In January 1884, a visit to three Wells, Stone & Co. camps indicated the harvest levels for the winter. It was reported that at "camp No. 1 (Gus Cribley foreman) they are putting in 75,000 feet daily, 8 teams at work; at A. Young's camp 65,000 feet; at a third camp 50,000 feet on 4 mile haul." Putting in nearly 200,000 board feet a day makes achieving a million board feet a week a reasonable goal.[12]

The company had two engines in service with fifteen cars each. In April, a third engine was added. With the rail connection now available at Meredith, no longer would the locomotives need to be hauled through the woods on plank roads.[13] [14]

As the Wright Lumber Company focused on new tracts to harvest, the importance of Achill diminished. On June 11, 1884, the

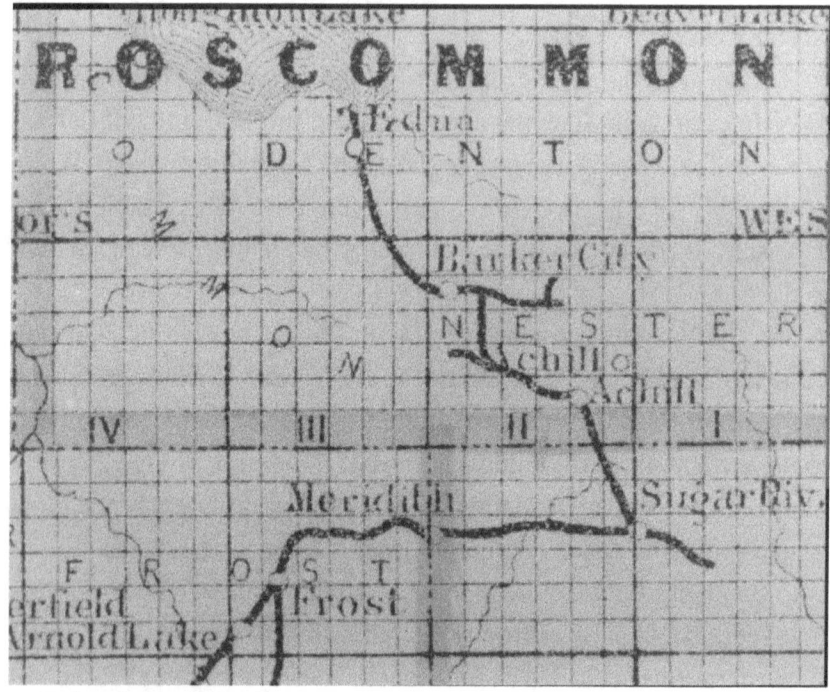

Railroad map of Michigan prepared for the Commissioner of Railroads by Henry S. Stebbins, map publisher, 264 Wabash Ave., Chicago, 1884.

Note the connection between the Roscommon Lumber Co. railroad and the A. W. Wright Lumber Company railroad. The Roscommon Lumber Company's headquarters camp is identified as Barker City.

first post office in West Nester Township was discontinued. Mail would be delivered at Meredith.[15]

The company headquarters was moved south toward the dams and the rail connection to Meredith. At this new location of Butman, a building boom was in effect in August. The new structures were a "large hotel, 30 X 60, three stories high, with wing 16 X 30, finished in good style from bottom to top; an engine house 40 X 110, with work shop connection; also a large store and several dwellings."[16] [17]

This development around Butman and the closing of the post office at Achill, prompted the establishment of the Butman post office on August 11, 1884.[18] [19]

As the rail connection at Meredith grew in importance, the company began construction of a large store there in November that by December was operating and managed by Nat Wright.[20] [21]

When the shanty boys headed into the woods in Roscommon County for the winter of 1884–85, monthly wages for common laborers were "$15 to $20; for scalers, cooks, foremen etc., $30 to $50; for tote teamsters and choppers, $20 to $30."[22]

Though the Wright Lumber Company would expand their railroad lines and put up additional buildings on the farms, the most striking news of the year was that the company had severed the railroad connection to the Roscommon Lumber Company line by August of 1885. That connection was in section eight, just east of Headquarters Lake. With the abandonment of the northern portion of the original Lake Thomas and Tittabawassee Railroad in Nester Township, the company's work was nearly finished in this portion of the township.[23] [24] [25]

While the company was almost finished harvesting its pine on the lands made accessible by the original rail line to Lake Thomas, Rollway Lake, Doyle Lake and Young Lake, they were not yet done in the southern part of the township. As we will see in chapter ten, the company planned a new route to enter the township.

The Wright Lumber Company would spend the years 1886 through 1893 focused on removing its timber, as well as others, from lands in Gladwin and Clare Counties and also in Roscommon Township. The company would build rail lines to the southeast, northwest and north of Meredith as well as off its main line between Meredith and Butman.

This map shows the railroad network in West Nester and Sherman Township circa 1884. The red lines are the Roscommon Lumber Company's. The blue lines are the Nester/Wright lines. The pink line is the Wright Lumber Company line to Meredith. The earliest reported dates of operation are noted. For the Roscommon Lumber Company specific branch dates are not available but the overall years of operation were 1882-87.

The connection line running south from section 8 was used by both companies. It gave the Roscommon Lumber Company access to its timber in section 29. Of course, it was also the final link connecting Prudenville with Meredith.

By August of 1893, the company was removing its tracks that connected Butman with Meredith and were sending the engines, equipment, and crews to Saginaw.[26]

It had taken only about 16 years, from the fall of 1877 to August 1893, and the great harvest of pine, utilizing the rail connection to the Sugar River, was over. It was the blink of an eye.

CHAPTER 9

The Roscommon Lumber Company

Besides the Nester operation and its successor, the only other significant lumber operator in West Nester during the pine era was the Roscommon Lumber Company. Unlike Nester's logs, though, the Roscommon Lumber Company's timber was sent to Muskegon. However, like Nester, the Roscommon Lumber Company depended on an isolated railroad to bring its logs to the nearest water substantial enough to float them to the mill, in this case Houghton Lake.

The Roscommon Lumber Company was a half million-dollar corporation organized in 1882 by Healy Cady Akeley of Grand Haven, where the company had its offices. Besides Akeley, other investors included Charles Boyden, also of Grand Haven, and Samuel B. Barker, George Sinclair, Thomas Morris, all of Chicago, as well as Charles B. Field. James Danhof was the secretary.[1][2][3][4][5]

H. C. Akeley (1836–1912) was born in Vermont and was fatherless by the age of nine. He labored on the family farm while attending public school. Seeking to establish a career for himself, for two summers he did survey work and read law. Eventually he attended Poughkeepsie Law School and was admitted to the bar in 1857. In

1858, Akeley moved to Grand Haven, Michigan, to practice law. After serving in the Union Army, he returned to Grand Haven and began a career which involved law, public service, and lumber.[6]

One of the original and most substantial purchases of pineland the company made that included acreage in West Nester was in the

Healy Cady Akeley (1836–1912)

spring of 1882 from Henry Stephens & Co. of St. Helen (map, p. 64). The purchase price was "$375,000, one third cash and balance in six and 12 months. The tract embraces 7,800 acres." This represented a $250,000 profit for Stephens after holding these lands for only two years.[7 8]

Proceeding with alacrity typical of the time but difficult to comprehend today, by March of 1883, it had "eight miles of railroad track besides branches and sidings." The company was averaging

200,000 feet a day into Houghton Lake on trains carrying 20,000 feet per load. By October of 1884, the company was expanding its railroad and planning on running trains night and day. It had 130 men employed by December of 1884.[9]

To facilitate the flotation of their logs, in early 1883 the company rebuilt a dam on the Muskegon River a short distance from the lake. This dam was originally erected by the S. C. Hall Lumber Company. The resulting increase in the level of the lake flooded out one of the original area farmers who had 680 acres on the lake. The company was immediately enjoined to cease construction and was sued for damages. The case would eventually arrive at the Michigan Supreme Court during January 1886 as Stone vs. Roscommon Lumber Co. and others. The complainant's case was affirmed with costs.[10]

Early on, the Roscommon Lumber Company's railroad was referred to as the Houghton Lake & Barker City Railroad. This followed the nomenclature of the times for some of the early lumbering railroads that had the terminus and an interior location or river in the name. The Lake George & Muskegon River Railroad and the Lake Thomas & Tittabawasse River Railroad are two earlier examples. This railroad would later be referred to as the Charles B. (C. B.) Field's Railroad, or simply the Field's Railroad.

The early name of the headquarters camp (Barker City) is believed to be taken from one of the partners, Samuel Burns Barker. His Chicago firm, S.B. Barker & Co., was acclaimed as "remarkable even in this, the greatest lumber market in the world." This expansive yard, described in 1891, had "track room for seventy-five cars to load at one time" with "sixty cars having been handled in ten hours." With lumber arriving via the Great Lakes, there was "dock room for twelve vessels to unload simultaneously."[11]

By 1891, Barker was also "the principal stockholder in the Itasca Lumber Company, of Minneapolis." This corporation owned "a large body of pine land in Minnesota, estimated capable of

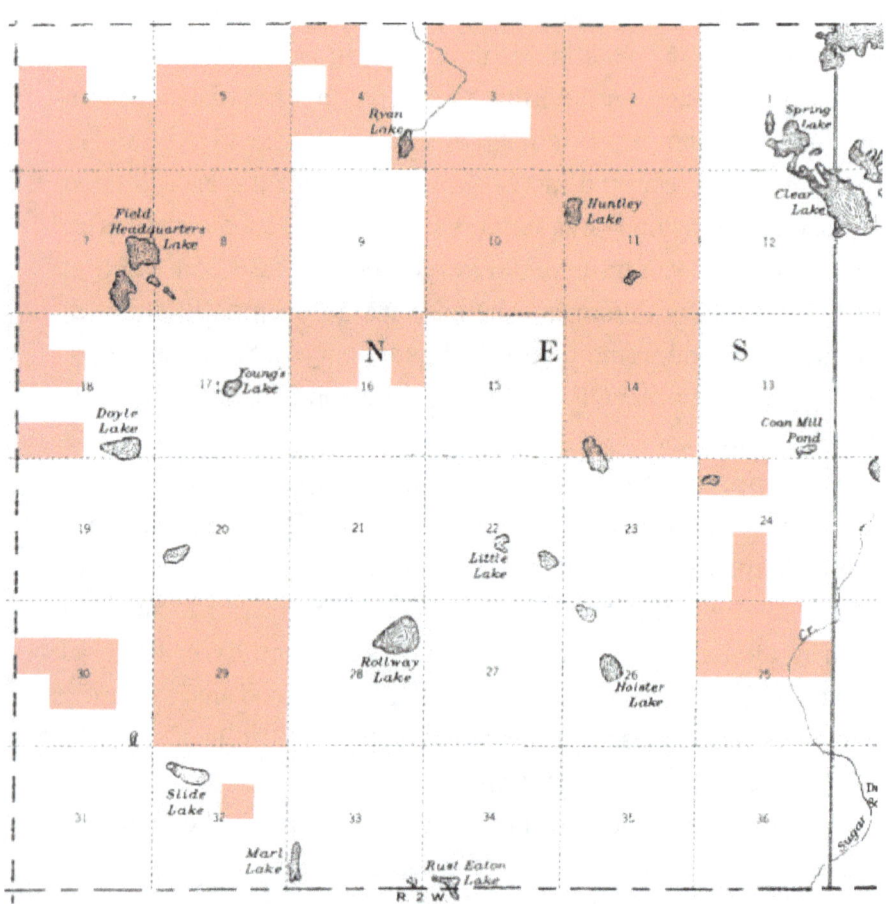

In the spring of 1882, the Roscommon Lumber Company purchased the highlighted parcels, along with other lands not in West Nester Township, from Henry Stephens & Co. of St. Helen.

producing seven hundred million to eight hundred million feet of logs." He also owned "about four thousand acres of hardwood lands in Charlevoix county" and interest in "several thousand acres of pine lands in Louisiana." It is doubtful if he ever visited his namesake "city" in Nester Township.[12]

In 1884, the Houghton Lake & Barker City railroad was described as 12 miles long and standard gauge. It was built of 30-lb T rail with its steepest grade being 75 feet over one-half mile. Two locomotives were in service, one an 18 ton from H.K. Porter & Co. and the other a 27 ½ ton from Brooks Locomotive Works. Other equipment included 30 cars from the Russell Wheel & Foundry Co. The company averaged 200,000 feet per day with the average haul being 11 miles. The average speed was 15 miles per hour with loads averaging 1,850 feet per car.[13]

The main line of the railroad ran from Prudenville to the company's primary camp at Headquarters Lake. At Prudenville "the track was extended some 40 to 50 rods out into the lake on spiles on which stringers are laid." Proceeding south from Prudenville, the old railroad bed can still be seen on the west side of M-18 and then as it nears Mid-Forest Lodge on the east side of the highway. Eventually, since Barker City was the headquarters camp (hence the name of the lake), it was called Field's Headquarters after the company's general manager, Charles B. Field. Though modern maps refer to the lake as Headquarters Lake, earlier maps from the twenties and thirties still identified it as Field Headquarters Lake.[14]

John W. Fitzmaurice, a "Hospital Agent," gives us a brief first-person account of Charlie Field's headquarters camp. His four-year career would take him to over 400 lumber camps selling "tickets" to the men, an early form of health insurance. Fitzmaurice made the twenty-mile tramp to Field's headquarters camp from Roscommon in time for supper and in hindsight complimented it as "one of the best provided camps in Michigan." He recalled that he was welcomed by "as good a lot of woodsmen as I ever had occasion to meet."[15]

Some years the company would sell its logs on the ice to parties in Muskegon. The logs were banked on the lake all winter and sold before the spring breakup. In early February 1884, it was reported that the firm had 30,000,000 feet, "most of which they have on the ice now." The following December, the company planned to have 25,000,000 on the ice. Again, they were selling to Muskegon parties and had "refused $11 per M for these logs on the ice." Not surprising, because the year before "they were worth $12 to $15."[16] [17]

Once the ice broke up, the logs still needed to be rafted to the outlet of Houghton Lake where the Muskegon Boom Company would assume control of all the logs. These logs from various operators were coming from Higgins Lake as well as Houghton Lake. In May of 1883, the Roscommon Lumber Company took on the job of driving Houghton Lake. The company had a small fleet of vessels to do the work. "The tugs Little Jake and Alice and four floats comprise the lake squadron with numerous accessories." Typically, the drive would be divided between the various companies. For example, in April of 1887, the *Roscommon News* revealed that "Charles Blanchard has secured the contract to drive Higgins Lake and the 'Cut' as far as Marl Lake, from which point C. B. Fields will have charge."[18] [19]

In April of 1886, the Roscommon Lumber Company "employed 300 men, and put in about a million and a half logs [feet] a week in Houghton Lake." By April they had 23,000,000 feet of logs in the lake and were planning to be running their railroad all summer. The company also announced that they would be "cutting without doubt the two best sections of pine timber that stands in Michigan, one estimated to contain twenty-eight million feet and the other twenty-five million." The season prior they had sold their logs for $12.00 straight. At that price, these two sections would produce logs worth a staggering $336,000 and $276,000 respectively.[20] [21]

Like Nester, the Roscommon Lumber Company also moved timber for other concerns. When fires broke out in May 1887, about "1,000,000 feet of hardwood logs owned by W.H. & F.A. Wilson, burned on the Roscommon Lumber company's logging road. Loss about $5,000." The Wilsons were the original land patentees of three parcels in West Nester Township (parts of sections 4, 30 & 36). This burnt timber may have been from their original holdings or even from newer purchases. The logs, being hardwoods, were to be railed out via Meredith, undoubtedly to their mill in Harrison.[22]

In their final season, Charles B. Fields reported that by May of 1887 the company had banked 57,000,000 feet of logs. The final figure reported in July was 70,215,000 feet of pine. The company had employed 700 men in this final push to conclude operations in West Nester. Having begun only five years prior and having harvested 175,000,000 feet, it was done in the state.[23] [24]

On August 3, the company sold its "logging railroad property, consisting of locomotives, and other personal property, for $30,000" to the Toledo, Ann Arbor & Northern Michigan Railway under a contract with the last payment to be made on October 15, 1887. However, it wasn't until June of 1888 that the company had "a large crew of men taking up the iron." There was "about 20 miles of track to be lifted."[25] [26]

C. B. Fields would leave the state and start his own lumber concern in Dry Run, Arkansas. He would proudly compete with Michigan lumber in the Chicago market and claim in October of 1889: "We are right after those Michigan lumbermen and we are getting our lumber into Michigan's territory."[27]

Seeing that the timber supply in the Muskegon drainage was diminishing, H. C. Ackeley had already made plans before the Roscommon Lumber Company was even done in the state. He organized the Itasca Lumber Company in Minneapolis, Minnesota, in 1886 and moved there the following year.[28]

The Roscommon Lumber Company lands in West Nester would not immediately revert to the state for tax delinquency, as was common. The land was sold to Hovey & McCracken in late 1888 and it was reported in the Roscommon paper in January 1889 that 8,500 acres were transferred.[29]

CHAPTER 10

The Last Train to Edna

For anyone familiar with Roscommon County, it is easy to recite two existing communities historically connected by a railroad to the rest of the state, those being Roscommon and St. Helen. These communities still retain that connection today. Doubtful few could suggest another existing community. However, as we have seen, by a curious combination of circumstances, and for only a few brief years, there in fact exists a third hamlet that was also tied to the outside world by rail.

As early as 1880, arrangements were under way for continuing the Budd Lake division (Harrison Branch) of the Flint & Pere Marquette Railroad and ultimately connecting it with Thomas Nester's railroad. It would be more than two years before construction of this branch would be approaching Nester's line (by then the Wright Lumber Company line). By August 1883, the work on this extension was reported to have "progressed finely during the past three weeks of dry weather." Railroad construction such as this extension was achieved with muscle power both human and equine. The contractor, M. Lally, had "about 230 Italians and 30 teams working" on the grade. The work was accomplished using principally "dump carts, dump cars, wheel scrapers and wheelbarrows."

Completion of the 20-mile new grade to the Wright Lumber Company's railroad was predicted to occur by September 30.[1][2]

This branch was winding its way toward the northeast corner of Clare County to what would become the rough-and-tumble

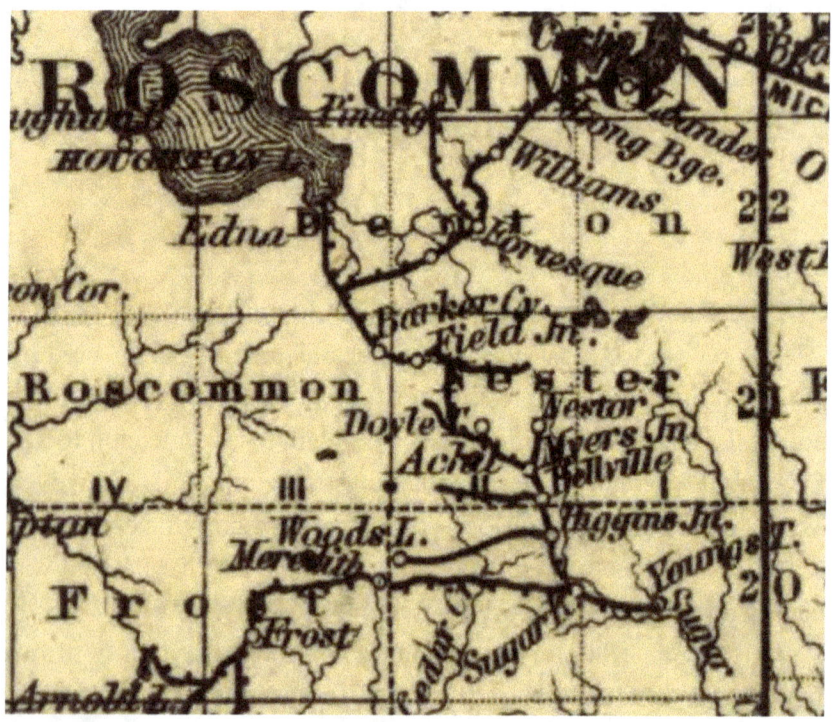

Colton's Map of Michigan showing the Toledo, Ann Arbor & North Michigan Railway and connecting lines. Published by G. W. & C. B. Colton & Co., New York, 1886.

Note: The connection between the Roscommon Lumber Company line and Fortesque cannot be confirmed on the ground.

town of Meredith. In October 1883, the *Gladwin County Record* announced that it "is expected that the Harrison branch of the Flint & Pere Marquette railroad will be connected with the A. W. Wright Lumber Company's road this week. The latter road connects with the road of the Roscommon Lumber Company, which extends to

Houghton Lake, and arrangements are to be made whereby lumber supplies can be shipped direct from the Saginaws to Houghton Lake over the roads named. The Harrison branch is 20 miles long, the A. W. Wright Lumber Company's road 14 miles and that of the Roscommon Lumber Company eight miles."[3]

This route was incredibly circuitous considering that Meredith lies directly south of this settlement on the east bay of Houghton Lake, now called Edna. Confusingly, this settlement had somewhat of an identity crisis. Originally, it was called Prudenville, until January of 1876, when the post office name was changed to Edna. The location reverted to its original appellation in January 1886.[4]

This original rail connection to Edna began at Meredith and followed the Wright line (today's Meredith Grade) east approximately to the Butman Township line in section 13 of Sherman Township, near where the Sugar River crosses F-97 today. From there, the route turns northwest to a junction south of Lake Thomas (present day Atchel Lake) and continued northwest past Rollway Lake, eventually turning north in section 20. Proceeding north, the Wright line connected with the Roscommon Lumber Company line. This line angled west past the Headquarters Lake and there, turning northwest again, it left West Nester and followed present day M-18 to Houghton Lake (map, p. 58). With this amalgam of railroads, Edna (Prudenville) now had its rail link to the outside world.

In November of 1883, the Gladwin paper enthused about this development: "Passenger coaches are seen daily on the A. W. Wright Co's road in north Gladwin. Regular freight trains every other day. Who says Gladwin County cannot boast of railroad communication with the outside world?" Remarkably, it would be four more years before the city of Gladwin had its own railroad.[5] [6]

Optimism concerning the permanence of the connection was rife. In 1884, it was announced that there "is to be a new depot erected at Houghton Lake, on the Roscommon lumber company's railroad, and regular freight business carried on." Why shouldn't the citizens of Edna be hopeful? Certainly, they believed the claim that with the "track being a standard gauge, nothing prevents a lively traffic."[7]

But the rail connection to Edna, as mentioned, was transient, and in less than two years it was imperiled. By June of 1885 it was reported that "Wells, Stone & Co. are about to take up their railroad from Meredith towards Houghton Lake and that C. B. Fields will regrade the road and the F. & P. M. will re iron *[sic]* it, after which a train will run through to Houghton Lake." By late summer it was noted that the "proposed scheme of running a passenger train from Meredith to Houghton lake over the A. W. Wright Lumber Co's logging road has failed. The company has removed the iron from their main line north of the Meredith branch, thus breaking up the rail connection between Meredith and Houghton lake." West Nester was now stripped of the railroad lines that were begun in the fall of 1877 by Thomas Nester and which had carried away the lumber of a significant portion of the southern part of the township.[8] [9]

Apparently, Prudenville (Edna changed its name back to Prudenville in January 1886) did not stay detached from the outside world for long. The following spring (1886) it was claimed that the interior termination of the Roscommon Lumber Company's was at Meredith. Could this be? Though the claim may have been early, by June the Gladwin paper confirmed that "Field's lumber road from Houghton Lake is now connected with the F. & P. M. at Meredith" and that the "first train passed over the road last week." Prudenville had a respite from isolation. And the Roscommon Lumber Company found that rail linkage to Meredith was crucial enough to contribute to an alternate route. But this "western route" was not the exclusive development of the Roscommon Lumber Company.[10] [11]

It is uncertain how the Roscommon Lumber Company and the Wright Lumber Company divided the cost and work of this "western route." This route crossed lands owned by both companies and joined the Wright Lumber Company line to Meredith in Gladwin

County. Additionally, the one major spur off this "western route" also crossed over a mix of both companies' properties.

This new line started in section 18 of T. 20 N., R. 2 W., leaving the Wright company's main railroad that ran between Meredith and the dam near Butman. From there it proceeded roughly north through sections 7 and 6 of the same township. Continuing north it entered West Nester Township, passing through sections 31, 30, 19, and 18 and joining the Roscommon Lumber Company line in section 7 just west of the Field Headquarters Lake. This path, and subsequent spurs, gave the Roscommon Lumber Company access to its timber in sections 18, 29, 30 and 32. Similarly, it gave the Wright Lumber Company access, again with future spurs, to sections 19, 28, 30, 32 and 33. This western route curved advantageously for the Wright Lumber Company at its main spur in section 30 of West Nester Township and at its junction in section 18 of Sherman Township. In both incidences, the track curves toward the route headed to the Sugar River and not toward Houghton Lake in section 30 of West Nester Township and not toward Meredith in section 18 in Sherman Township. Had these two junctions curved in opposite directions it would have been advantageous to trains of the Roscommon Lumber Company. All this suggests that though the Roscommon Lumber Company regained access to Meredith by rail, the construction was made to the Wright Lumber Company's preference.

Over the years, while this new rail link to Houghton Lake existed, several excursions were provided to area residents. The first of three notable undertakings occurred in the summer of 1886. On Saturday, July 18, the train left Harrison bound for Prudenville with a "large crowd of sightseers and pleasure seekers, among whom were the Band, Fire Company, and numerous prominent citizens."

After passing through northern Clare County to Meredith the train proceeded through West Nester to Prudenville. "After lunch about 200 boarded the steamer Little Jake and accompanied by every boat

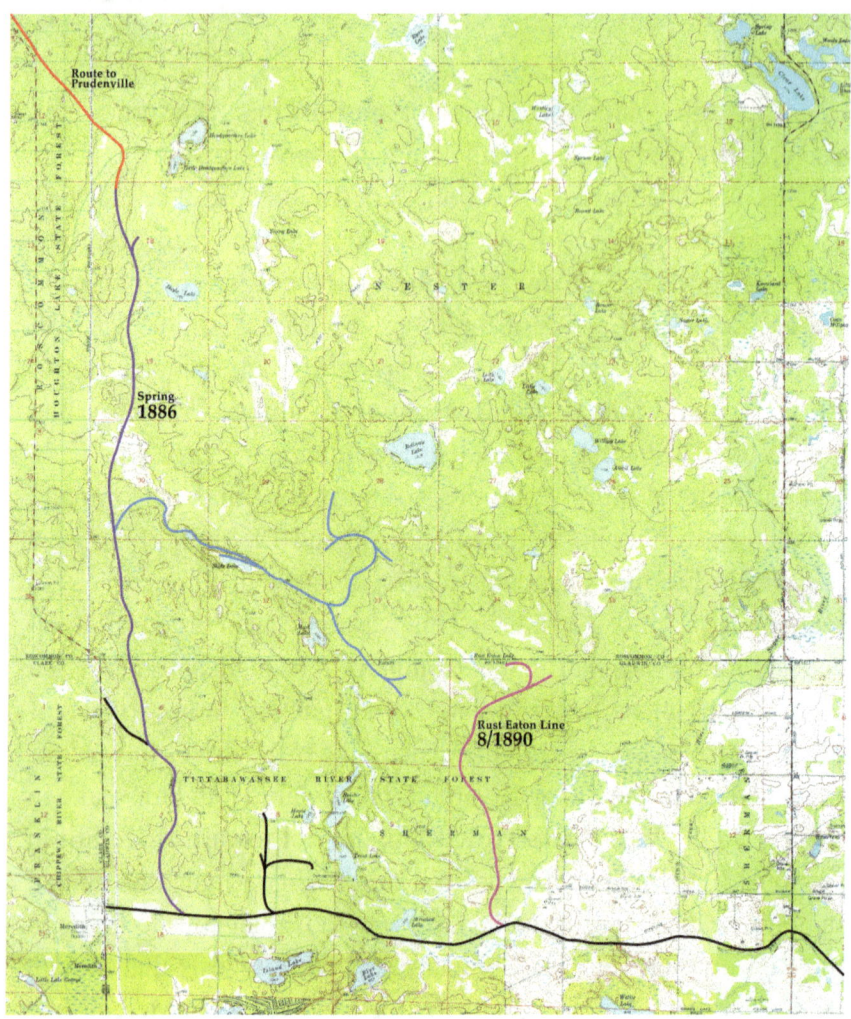

"The Western Route"

After the original rail connection between Prudenville and Meredith was disconnected, the "Western Route" was quickly laid. It certainly helped the Roscommon Lumber Company for it gave it the access again to Meredith and the Harrison Branch of the Flint & Pere Marquette RR. This connection was reported in the spring of 1886. This route is shown in purple. The line crossed both the Roscommon Company's and the Wright Lumber Company's property. The blue branch line also crossed both company's property. The black line is the Wright Company's Meredith line as well as two branches that crossed only its property. The pink line is the Rust Eaton Company railroad branch. The other lines of the Roscommon Lumber Company and the older lines of the Thomas Nester Railroad have been removed to highlight the Western Route.

at Prudenville filled with members of the party enjoyed a ride on the lake. Supper was partaken of at the Pruden House and Harcourt's Hotel after which the trip concluded with a grand dance at the hall in the Harcourt Hotel which continued until 12 o'clock p.m. when the company embarked on the train for their respective homes." This trip was viewed as an "immense success" and all heartily enjoyed the hospitality. It was hoped that trips such as this would be a precursor to regular rail service including both passenger and mail.[12]

The succeeding summer (1887) there would be two similar trips on this hodgepodge railroad.

The first outing of the year was on Sunday, May 22. "J. F. Killorin and C. B. Fields gave a free excursion to a few of their friends over their railroads to Houghton Lake." The invited couples boarded the train at Butman and Meredith in the morning and arrived at Houghton Lake by 10:30 a.m. "At the lake they were joined by C. B. Fields who had everything in readiness for a grand good time." For dinner, the guests "found tables spread with everything the heart could wish." The early afternoon was spent on the water. The "steamer 'Little Jake' took the party over the lake a distance of about 40 miles, returning to Prudenville at 3 pm, where they took the train for home." The Gladwin guests thought "the affair one of the most enjoyable of the season."[13]

The second excursion was on Sunday, July 17, hosted by Mr. and Mrs. John F. Killorin. He was the superintendent of the Ammi W. Wright Lumber Company at Butman. "The party was made up of some 30 invited guests from Gladwin, Butman and Meredith." A morning rail ride to the lake was followed by lunch and "a ride in a huge scow, which had been fitted in bowery style by Chas. Field, and which was rowed around the lake by one of the Roscommon Lumber Co's tugs." The Gladwin party expressed "unbounded praise of the treatment received."[14]

Apparently, this was the farewell trip for the public because that same week the Roscommon Lumber Company announced its intentions to cease operations in the township. Undoubtedly, the trips that summer were made mindful of the fact that this unique opportunity to travel by rail through West Nester Township to Houghton Lake was short lived. Though it was the hope of the citizens of Prudenville to have permanent train service from Harrison, this would never materialize and the tenuous connection by rail would be permanently disjoined when the Roscommon Lumber Company ended its operation in Roscommon County late in the summer of 1887.

CHAPTER 11

The State Count

I n June of 1884, Patrick Kingsley, besides being an agent for St. Mary's hospital in Saginaw, selling early forms of health insurance, took on the task of enumerator for Nester Township during the state census of 1884.[1]

That census provides a timely glimpse of the township just as the Wright Lumber Company is about to abandon Achill and while the Roscommon Lumber Company is midway through their harvest. Kingsley was required to visit every dwelling and tabulate the occupants.

The census lists 31 occupied buildings. There is no indication that any lumber operations other than the Wright Lumber Company and the Roscommon Lumber Company were harvesting timber in the township. The Hauptman Branch was years away from entering the township and occupations related to a lumber railroad, such as locomotive engineer, railroad fireman, railroad car inspector, and railroad worker, are scattered throughout 14 of the 31 buildings.

It is difficult to discern exactly which of these buildings are part of either operation. Unquestionably, the first buildings are the Wright Lumber Company's because in building three is listed John F. Killorin, railroad superintendent and a well-known and prominent Wright employee. Likewise, Charles B. Field is found in building twenty-nine. He oversaw the Roscommon Lumber Company operation.

Like the 1880 Federal Census, the view four years later finds mostly men in the woods. Of the 392 people enumerated, only 37 are women. Twenty of these are wives of the most skilled laborers. Men with vocations such as cook, carpenter, locomotive engineer, millwright, bookkeeper, railroad fireman, railroad car inspector, baker, railroad foreman and lumber operator were allowed to have their wives in the woods. The remaining females were fifteen daughters, a servant and one related minor.

Not surprisingly, of the 355 men listed, 308 are under the age of 40. Only twenty-one of the "older" men were common shanty boys. The rest of these seniors held positions with the railroads or were cooks, blacksmiths, carpenters, sailors, teamsters, millwrights, log scalers, foremen or head lumber operators.

If young boys dreamed of working in the big woods of Michigan, those young boys that fulfilled that dream in Nester Township were predominantly born in Canada, for they provided over 40% of the labor force. The only other significant foreign country of nativity was Ireland. For the native born, Michigan dominated with over 17% born Wolverines. New York, Pennsylvania, and Massachusetts make up the only other states with significant numbers.

Only one farmer and his family are identified in the township. This farmer's home was visited, by the enumerator, right among the lumber company buildings. Perhaps he worked a small company farm, supplying fresh vegetables and meat for the crew.

Schedule four of the census summarized all manufacturing in the township. Only the Wright Lumber Company is examined. This schedule gives an account of labor, wages, equipment, etc. The Wright Lumber Company reported an average of 300 employees. They worked 12-hour days from approximately May through November and nine-hour days the remainder of the year. Skilled labor garnered $2.25 a day and unskilled only $1.25. The company reportedly paid out $20,000 in wages for the year. Three locomotives were in use.

Twenty thousand dollars does not account for 300 employees working six days a week. The total reported only accounts for about 51 employees at the lower wage level. It is impossible to reconcile these numbers.

CHAPTER 12

The Railroad from the East

A lfred Wright and Robert H. Weideman, partners in the firm Wright & Weideman, were among the earliest investors in Ogemaw County timberland. Soon after the arrival of the Jackson, Lansing & Saginaw Railroad into the county, this company began lumbering operations southwest of the city of West Branch. Though Wright died in 1873 and Weideman in 1882, the successor company, R. H. Weideman & Company, was critical in the inception of a new branch of the Jackson, Lansing & Saginaw Railroad.[1]

The Gladwin paper reported in October 1883 that "Weideman & Co. of East Saginaw have let the contract for the construction of a logging road, leaving the main line of the Mackinaw division of the Michigan Central two miles south of West Branch, and running nearly west 4 ½ miles into T. 21-1E. About 100 men are at work on the job." These new tracks were first referred to as the Weideman line or Weideman branch.[2]

By 1884, this line was at times also being cited as the Weideman & Hauptman Branch. Like Weideman, George N. Hauptman owned timberlands in Ogemaw County that were situated farther west in Edwards Township. Though the Michigan Central was constructing the branch, Weideman & Hauptman contributed the right of way, the ties and $10,000. Weideman & Hauptman also guaranteed that the lumber would be shipped to East Saginaw while the Michigan Central provided a special rate for these lumbermen. In July, the grading was near completion and by September the rails were being laid.[3] [4]

During the fall of 1887 an 8- to 10-mile extension of this branch was being planned to cross the remainder of Edwards Township and enter East Nester Township. It would snake its way west following the valley of the upper reaches of the west branch of the Tittabawassee River. Operating for Eddy, Avery & Eddy in East Nester Township, Charles Woods was already planning on utilizing this branch in the winter of 1887–8. By December of 1888, the now singularly labeled Hauptman Branch extended 15 miles. Wires were being strung to run the trains using telephone communication.[5] [6] [7]

The Hauptman Branch would not be further extended until the Michigan Central secured the contract from Jonathan Boyce, in August of 1890, to haul his timber from east Roscommon Township to his mill in Essexville. At this time, it was reported that the railroad was within six miles of the Boyce timber. This would place the terminus at the western extreme of East Nester Township, in the vicinity of Clear Lake.[8]

The railroad company now sought ownership of a strip of land to cross West Nester Township. The railroad would first need to enter section 12 of West Nester Township. The Ammi Wright Lumber Company owned this section and sold a right of way to the railroad in 1890. The railroad was granted a 100-foot-wide right of way across the section. It was stipulated that it would revert back to the grantor when it was no longer utilized by the railroad. The sale allowed for the Hauptman Branch to extend into West Nester Township. The railroad obtained similar rights from Hovey and McCracken, successors to the Roscommon Lumber Company, allowing the railroad to completely cross the township.[9]

Now in a rush of construction, the Hauptman Branch would be propelled across West Nester Township. In October of 1890, the *Gladwin County Record* revealed the following details: "A contract was signed last week by which John M. Lally of Detroit, is to construct a 12-mile extension to the Hauptman Branch of the Michigan Central railroad. This branch is a logging road branching off the main line of the Michigan Central at West Branch and running 12 miles back into the pine land known as the Hauptman district. This branch was built on a contract by Mr. Lally's father, seven years ago. The present extension, which will make the branch 24 miles long, penetrates what is known as the Boyce timber district, containing over 300,000,000 feet of standing pine. The road has been surveyed and work will be begun immediately. By this contract, Mr. Lally is to do all the work of constructing the road, except the laying of steel. Two hundred men and 75 teams will be set at work and an endeavor made to get as much of the work done as possible before January 1 next, as about that time the ground becomes so hard that little grading can be done."[10]

This extension entered West Nester Township just south of Clear Lake in section 12. Here the branch banked south to avoid the gradient in what is now an orchard and dropped into section 13 to find a more level path west. As construction of the Hauptman Branch proceeded, some of the grades of the Roscommon Lumber Company, abandoned only two years prior, were utilized once again. The branch proceeded west to the Field Headquarters Lake, then, unlike the old Roscommon Lumber Company track, headed southwest into Roscommon Township. By January 1891, trains were running across the township to the Boyce timber.[11]

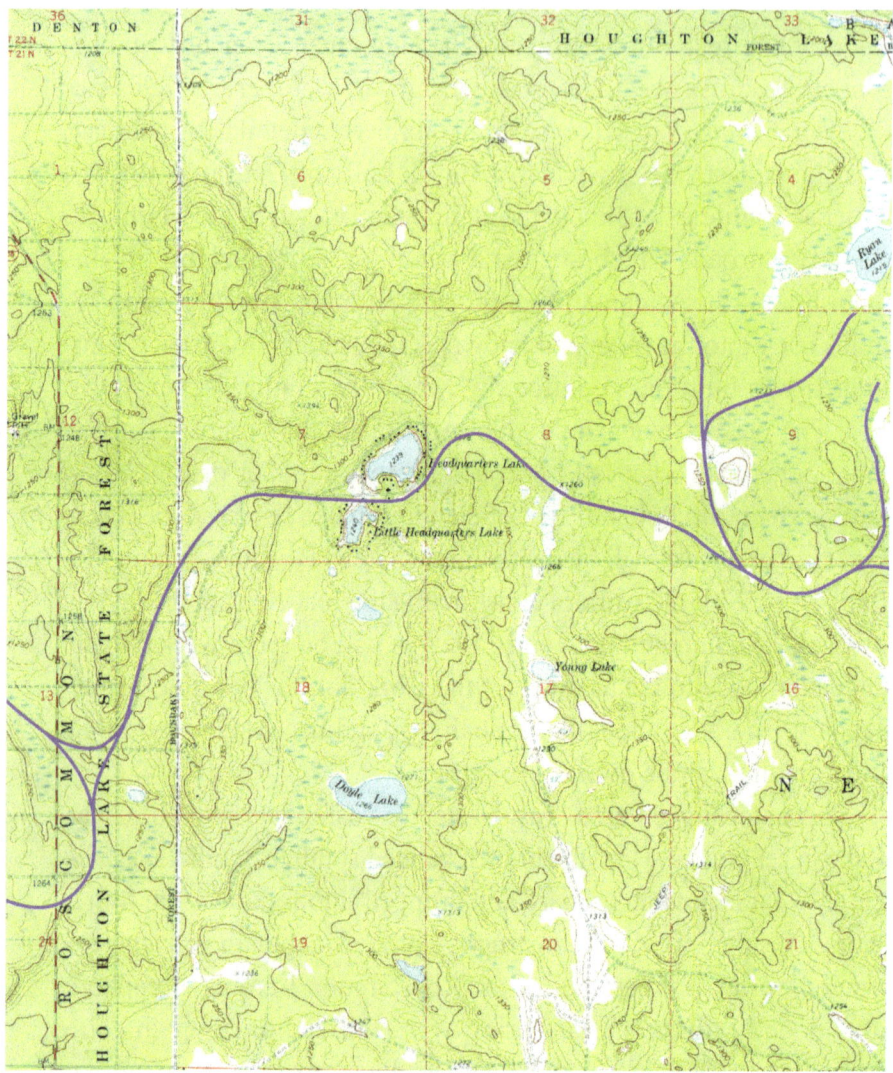

This two-page spread shows the northern half of West Nester Township. The Hauptman Branch railroad lines are shown in purple. The Hauptman Branch re-railed some of the old Roscommon Lumber Company's beds as it crossed the township. This branch operated in West Nester Township from 1890 until about 1901, though it serviced East Nester Township until about 1910.

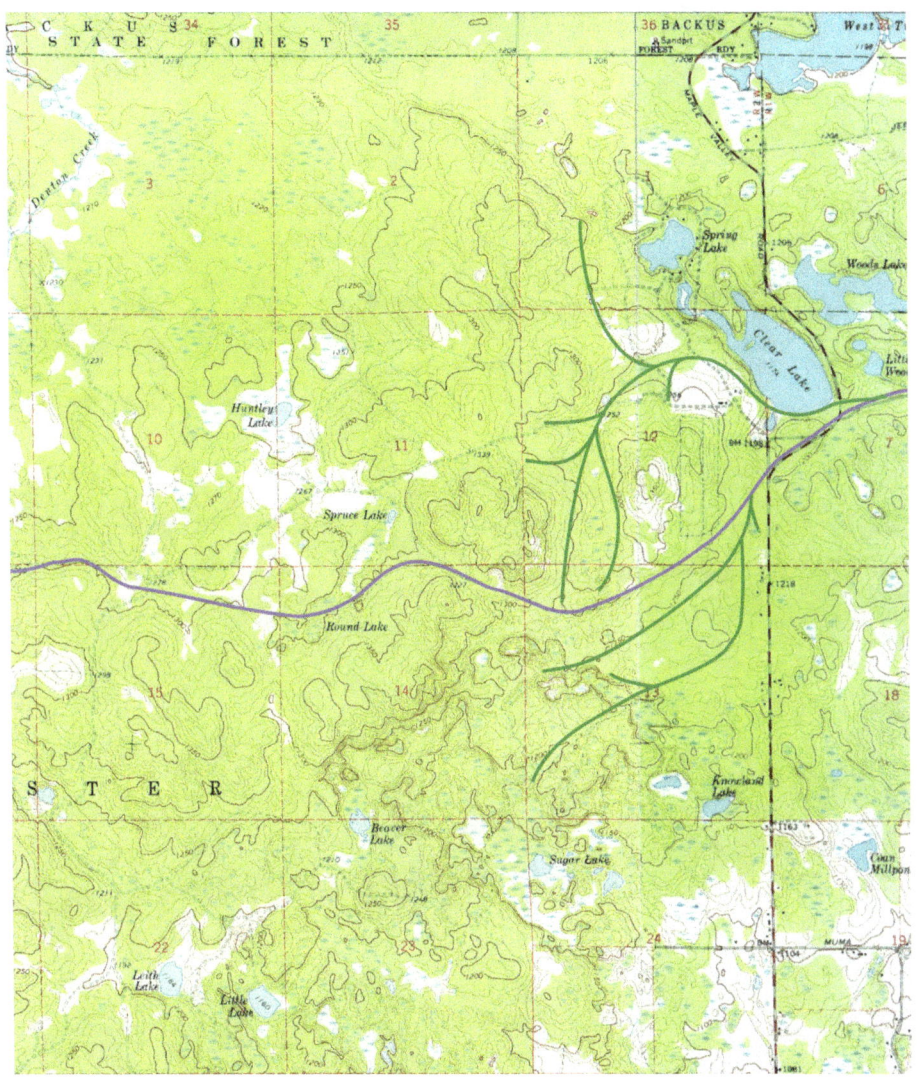

The Wright Lumber Company's railroad lines are shown in green.
The company utilized these lines from 1892 to 1896.

CHAPTER 13

The Clear Lake Harvest

T hough the pine timber had been removed from the old Roscommon Lumber Company lands along this new extension of the Hauptman Branch, the Wright Lumber Company had yet to harvest its pine in sections 1, 12, and 13 in West Nester Township. These lands were isolated, by ownership and topography, from their original railroad in the southern part of the township. Furthermore, the Wright Lumber Company had other pinelands to harvest in Gladwin and Clare Counties before needing to focus on these somewhat isolated sections in the northeast corner of West Nester Township. Perhaps the principals of the Wright Lumber Company foresaw the eventual extension of the Hauptman Branch and waited for its arrival.

Regardless, during the spring of 1892, the Wright Lumber Company was reported to be planning a spur line off the Hauptman Branch. By summer, it was building this spur and already had 1 million board feet harvested. It expected to finish these sections in three years, at which time it would have exhausted its Michigan timber. This spur left the Hauptman Branch in section 7 of East Nester Township and ran west to the south shore of Clear Lake (referred to as Wright Lake at the time). The rails then skirted the south edge of the lake, rising onto pilings along the high bank. Continuing to follow the edge of the lake, the tracks eventually rose on the west side and split, sending a line north into section 1 and another south into section 12 (map, p. 85).[1 2]

A year later, in June of 1893, the Ammi Wright Lumber Company was moving their headquarters from Butman to Roscommon County. The camp and headquarters are believed to have been located next to Clear Lake. For the 1893–4 season, harvesting along this new branch started on October 1, 1893, with the one camp in operation. It was planning to put in 15 million board feet.[3 4]

By the summer of 1894, the Wright Lumber Company had a hoister operating on Clear Lake and was adding a spur that left the Hauptman Branch in section 12 and headed south into section 13. It was sending two trains a day and a total of 20 million board feet to Saginaw. By summer's end, it was hauling 1 million board feet a week to Saginaw and had 8 million left in the lake. In late September, one half million board feet a day were coming down to Saginaw from its Clear Lake operation. The company estimated that the timber harvest here would last another two and a half years.[5 6 7 8]

The following winter of 1894–5, the company put in another 20–25 million board feet. This timber was stored in the lake and eventually hoisted out and shipped to Saginaw. Only 7 million feet of this harvest were still in the lake by August of 1895. That month, the company was cutting 3 million board feet a month with 125 men in camp. This number of men may have represented two camps once the additional spur into section 13 was in place.[9 10 11]

The Wright Lumber Company had become an extraordinarily efficient enterprise, handling everything from the harvest to the final marketing of lumber. One example of this took place in October of 1895, when it "filled an order for large Norway timber in four days after it was taken, the logs being brought from Roscommon [County], over a hundred miles distant from the mill, by the Michigan Central railroad."[12]

The 1895–6 season would bring an end to the Wright Lumber Company's Clear Lake operation and exhaust its "timber on the Hauptman Branch." By January, it was sleighing 400,000 feet a week to the Wright Branch of the Hauptman. In April, the estimate was for 25 million to be sent down the Hauptman Branch to Saginaw. Fires damaged standing timber of several concerns on the Hauptman in June, including the Wright Lumber Company's, accelerating the need to harvest the remaining standing timber. The final push to get the timber down the Hauptman Branch was a reported 600,000 board feet per week.[13] [14] [15] [16] [17] [18]

This timeframe for the end of the Clear Lake timber harvest matches well with tax records. The Wright Lumber Company owed back taxes in Section 1 starting in 1895, presumably the harvest was over in this section and the company discontinued any tax payments. For the more critical Section 12, which included the headquarters camp, the lake and hoister and its main spur, taxes were paid through 1896, the last year of operation.[19]

In 1892, the Wright Lumber Company had predicted that these Clear Lake sections would be cleared up in three years "when all its Michigan timber will be exhausted." This prediction was early by only a year. In 1897, its Saginaw mill did not operate, and in 1898, the planing mill would be out of commission as soon as what stock remained was run through. Apparently, the Clear Lake timber would be some of the last company logs processed through the Wright mill. The Wright mill and earlier versions (the original mill burned down in 1865) had been an enduring presence in Saginaw. Dating back to 1863, the Wright mill (new and old) "manufactured approximately a grand total of 620,208,000 feet of pine lumber."[20] [21] [22] [23]

CHAPTER 14

Pernicious Pines

T hough the invasion by lumbermen into West Nester Township is only an imperfect military analogy, there were noteworthy similarities. As in any military campaign, death, let alone injury, was a frequent visitor to the lumber camps. As is still the case today, the felling of huge overhead giants was one of the deadliest occupations.

During the period from 1878 to 1889 the bulk of timber was harvested from West Nester. Examining this period reveals a surprising number of fatalities and injuries especially considering the somewhat seasonal population.

A sample of the alarming rate of mortality in the Michigan forests was noted in mid-March 1880. Sixty-six men had already met their deaths in the pinewoods of Michigan. A similarly shocking statistic was reported in early January 1884. In one previous week that season, "ten men and one women *[sic]* were killed in the pineries of northern Michigan."[1] [2]

Imagine today if any Michigan industry were reporting such figures. For comparison, in 2012 there were a total of 26 MIOSHA-related deaths in Michigan. Adjusted for population, the number of occupational deaths should have been only a little more than four for the whole year of 1880, not the astonishing total of 66 deaths, reported just from the lumber industry.

Causes of death included falling limbs, falling timber, rolling logs and, with the introduction of the steam locomotive into the pineries, trains and their rolling stock. Truly, these agents of mortality were common, and the newspapers of the day are replete with such incidents. But there were also less predictable means of perishing in the pineries and below are two examples of rather unconventional fatalities.

The colorful and picturesque image of the lumber woods evaporates quickly when an industrial fatality of the times is reviewed. On Sunday, March 16, 1884, brakeman Jay Arnot was gruesomely killed while attending his job on the last train for the week heading to the Sugar River for the Wright Lumber Company. It was Sunday morning about 4:00 a.m. "when the binder chain broke on his car, and in passing through a cut a log was caught by one end and upended, striking Arnot and knocking him from the train, under which he rolled and 16 cars passed over his body, cutting him into shreds. His head and a small portion of his body was all that could be secured for burial, the remainder having been crushed and mangled to a jelly, covering the cars and track for some distance." He was 21 years old, married and father of an 18-month-old son.[3]

During the prior summer, another unusual and lethal accident occurred on the Wells, Stone & Co. railroad in Nester Township. It was Saturday afternoon, August 4, 1883, and three employees, Philip Beard, Fred Oulett and Abraham Code, were manning a portable engine for sawing wood. At about 2:00 p.m. the boiler exploded, killing all three men. "Just before it occurred one of the men asked Philip Beard, the engineer what was the matter of the engine. Hardly were the words said before the boiler exploded with a terrific force, throwing a young man named Samuel McLellan full forty feet away" reported the Gladwin paper. The funerals were hurried due to the condition of the bodies.[4]

A complete list of fatalities attributable to the Nester/Wright and Roscommon Lumber Company operations that occurred over this time period (1878–1889) is impossible to establish. Nonetheless, the following reports lend some insight into the deadly nature of late 19th century commercial lumbering.

On Saturday, February 19, 1881, Owen Walsh was killed while working on Nester's banking ground. His remains were taken home to Quebec by his brother. Two months later, Simon Outerkirk was struck by a limb and died after being taken to West Branch for care. He was about 25 years old and from Montreal. Work was no less dangerous at the Roscommon Lumber Company. A brakeman, John Hamerin, was killed on Friday, May 16, 1884, having been run over by the train. In October of 1885, another Roscommon Lumber Company employee, John Merkly, "was instantly killed while coupling cars, catching his head just back of the ears and smashing his skull and causing instant death." He was Canadian and between 25 and 30 years old.[5] [6] [7] [8]

In December of 1885, a Wright Lumber Company employee, John McMann, was killed loading cars. Wright lost another man on March 10, 1886, a chopper killed by a falling tree. According to the Gladwin paper, the "tree was about to fall and the unfortunate man was trying to get out of reach as he supposed, when the tree fell in a direction not calculated upon, and striking him across the shoulders, killed him instantly."[9] [10]

As the pace of the harvest intensified for the Roscommon Lumber Company, fatalities followed suit. Another woodsman, Francis Budd of Harrison, lost his life coupling cars on May 12, 1886. Similar to a previous fatality, he "was caught between two logs projecting over the ends of the cars." On December 20 of the same year, a shanty boy hailing from Cleveland, Ohio, lost his life working out of one of C. B. Field's camps.[11] [12]

On December 3, 1888, one death occurred that exemplifies the bright promises that woodsman wages could provide an industrious young man and the tragic risks that could dash away their fruition. "Monday morning Michael O'Shea who was employed in loading cars on the Wright logging road, started for work in his usual health. A car had been loaded, when in binding the logs gave way, and O'Shea was caught and crushed under their cruel sway." He was 22 years of age and had laid up $500, which represented close to two years of wages.[13]

Accidents both minor and serious were so common as to preclude a detailed listing. Typical injuries were limbs crushed or broken while handling logs and rolling stock. Injuries could be life changing. One such incident occurred in April of 1881 at Charles Woods's camp: "A man by the name of Mat Burns was caught between two logs while breaking a rollway, and the lower part of his abdomen crushed in a horrible manner, causing paralysis in the legs and lower parts of his body."[14]

"A Frenchman, employed at the A. W. Wright Lumber Co.'s camp, got his leg caught in a rope used for letting cars down a hill, and was badly mangled," was the report from the *Gladwin County Record* in December of 1889. Like so many other shanty boys, he "was taken to St. Mary's hospital at East Saginaw," still alive at last account.[15]

Death did not distinguish between man or beast and though many stories of livestock losses from train collisions or disease were reported, one event, fatal to a pair of horses, stands out. Lake Thomas, like most small lakes in the pineries, was used for log storage. In the winter, pairs of horses would haul loads directly onto the ice and unload their logs. On Tuesday, January 13, 1880, at Lake Thomas, "a valuable span of horses belonging to Thomas Nester were drowned in the lake. The team had been driven upon the lake with a load of logs, and just as the binder was taken from the load, the sleighs sank through the ice, and pulled the horses with them into some 40 feet of water."[16]

For the shanty boy, work in the woods might last one season or many. Most would walk out of the woods with money for their family or to buy a farm. For some though, it was a quick trip south to Saginaw for medical care or burial.

CHAPTER 15

Lally's Wye

For a logging railroad isolated deep in the woods, a wye or Y facilitated the flow of trains from any of three approaches, allowed for trains to change directions, enabled trains to reconfigure the order of their cars, and even permitted them to change positions relative to one another. One such "Y" was located just outside West Nester Township and was a noted location along the Hauptman Branch as it entered the Boyce timber in Roscommon Township.

Though the Y is not located inside of West Nester Township, it is worth mentioning here. The Y is situated southwest of the headquarters gate of Mid-Forest Lodge. At the gate, the club road is following the abandoned railroad bed of the Hauptman Branch. The trail continues following the railroad bed until just reaching the northeast corner of the Y.

It is an easy walk to navigate the complete triangle delineated by this historic Y, for it is all contained in the SW¼ of section 13, of east Roscommon Township. Evidence of some of the old buildings and associated apple trees is concealed just north of the road after it turns due west to reach M-18. Trains coming from the east on the Hauptman Branch could proceed on either the north or south branch of the Y and penetrate the Boyce timber. Trains could also move from either of the branches to the other by means of a section of track that created the Y or triangular feature.

This Y was in service for approximately 12 years (1890–1901). It received its name from the Detroit railroad contractor that built this extension of the Hauptman Branch across West Nester Township, John M. Lally.

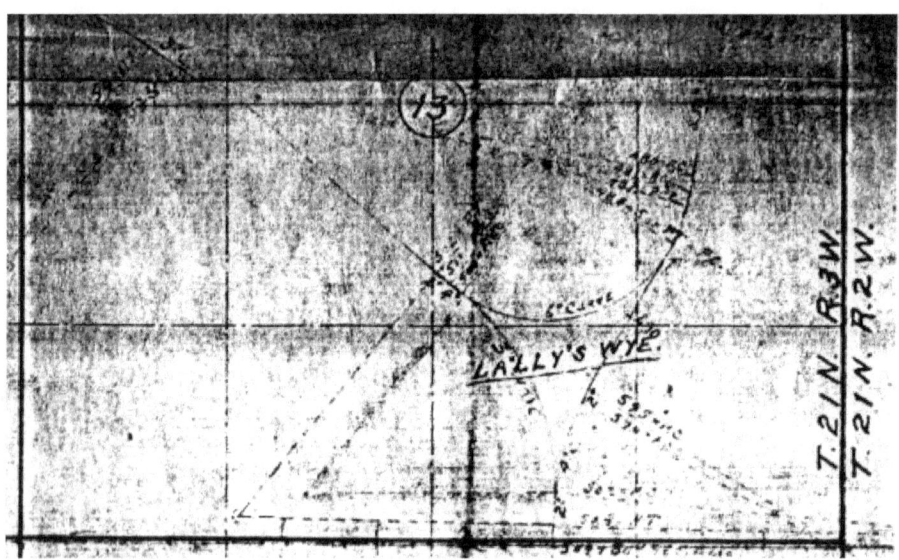

Map of Lally's Y located in the SW quarter of section 13, T. 21 N., R. 3 W. This drawing is part of the construction map of the Boyce Lines of the Hauptman Branch.

Image courtesy of the Clarke Historical Library, Central Michigan University.[1]

Undoubtedly due to both its importance to train traffic and its proximity to the Midland & Houghton Lake Road, Lally's Y was an attractive location for a variety of businesses and the rare settler. By 1893 Rachel Meister and her son Samuel had established a shingle mill at Lally's Y. Being dealers in second-hand equipment in Bay City, they also leased Jonathan Boyce such items as a portable boiler and engine and a Scotch boiler for his headquarters camp. Unfortunately, the mill and a boarding house burned down when fires swept through parts of Roscommon and Nester Townships in May 1893.[2][3]

Even as late as 1899 entrepreneurs were still gambling on the permanence of the Hauptman Branch. That year it was reported that, "Billy Harcourt has started business near the 'Y' as restaurateur and lodger."[4]

From the Y, occasional reports were sent to the Gladwin paper describing the news along the terminus of the Hauptman Branch. News from the logging camps, the amount of timber remaining, the sale of timber lands, the status of the Hauptman Branch itself (when switches and sidetracks were being removed), reports of mills being established, as well as the news from Denton Township, were all topics covered from Lally's Y. As the timber diminished, so did these curious updates from the western extremity of the Hauptman Branch.

Soon after the Hauptman Branch reached across West Nester Township and entered Roscommon Township, the Meister family established a mill on Lally's Y. The family patriarch Richard died in 1887 and his wife, Rachel, and son, Samuel, ran this business, as well as a machine shop in Bay City that manufactured boilers and engines.

Image courtesy of the Clarke Historical Library, Central Michigan University.[5]

CHAPTER 16

Old Nolan

T raversing West Nester Township beginning in 1890, the Hauptman Branch became the township's transportation pipeline. With the Hauptman Branch in place, it was only a matter of time before a new post office would be established in the township.

William Finley (1850–1923) applied for the new office, as well as to be its first postmaster, in May of 1891. Mail would arrive via Meredith. The requested name of the new office was Nolan. The office opened in June of that year. It was claimed that the new post office would serve 300 people.[1]

This new post office would be in an old location. The office would be four rods north of the Hauptman Branch in the southeast corner of section seven. This was the old Field's Headquarters of the Roscommon Lumber Company.[2]

The Nolan post office would remain at this location until September of 1899 when it was moved to East Nester Township with Edward Coan as postmaster.[3]

The township officials during the early years of Nolan's existence included William Finley, Rufus C. Huntley (1855–1937), Alexander Robinson (1852–1916) and Nathaniel T. McDonald (1842–1916). Unfortunately, these four officials came to bring an

No. 1011.   (LOCATION PAPER.)

Post Office Department,

OFFICE OF THE FIRST ASSISTANT P. M. GENERAL,

Appointment Division,

WASHINGTON, D. C., **MAY 5** 1891 _____, 18 __ .

Sir: Before the Postmaster General decides upon the application for the establishment of a post office at _Nester_ , County of _Roscommon_ , State of _Michigan_ , it will be necessary for you to carefully answer the subjoined questions, get a neighboring postmaster to certify to the correctness of the answers, and return the location paper to the Department, addressed to me. If the site selected for the proposed office should not be on any mail route now under contract, only a "Special Office" can be established there, to be supplied with mail from some convenient point on the nearest mail route by a special carrier (see section 733, Postal Laws and Regulations of 1887), for which service a sum equal to two-thirds of the amount of the salary of the postmaster at such office will be paid by the Department.

You should inform the contractor, or person performing service for him, of this application, and require him to execute the inclosed certificate as to the practicability of supplying the proposed office with mail, and return the same to the Department.

Very respectfully,

S. A. Whitfield

First Ass't Postmaster General.

To Mr. _____

care of the Postmaster of _____, who will please forward to him.

STATEMENT.   _Nolan._

The proposed office to be called _Nester Roscommon County M._

Select a short name for the proposed office, which, when written, will not resemble the name of any other post office in the State.

It will be situated in the _S. E._ quarter of Section _Seven_, Township _21_ (North or South), _North_ Range _West_ (East or West), _West_, in the County of _Roscommon_, State of _Michigan_.

It will be on or near route No. _____, being the route from _____ to _____, on which the mail is now carried _____ times per week.

Will it be directly on this route?—_Ans._ _No_

If not, how far from it?—_Ans._ _About seven miles_

If not on any route, is a "Special Office" wanted?—_Ans._ _Yes_ To be supplied from _Meredith Mich_

The name of the nearest office to the proposed one, on one side, is _____

Its distance is _____ miles in a _northeasterly_ direction from the proposed office.

The name of the nearest office, on the other side, is _Meredith_

Its distance is _six & one half_ miles in a _southern_ direction from the proposed office.

The name of the other nearest office to the proposed one is _____

Its distance by the most direct road is _sixteen_ miles in a _natural_ direction from the proposed office.

The name of the most prominent river near it is _____

The name of the nearest creek is _Hamilton_

The proposed office will be _here_ _____ miles from said river, on the _____ side of it, and will be _twelve_ _____ miles from said nearest creek, on the _South_ side of it.

The name of the nearest railroad is _Michigan Central Jackson Saginaw road_

If on the line of or near a railroad, on which side will the office be located; how far from the track, and what is, or will be, the name of the station?—_Ans._ _____ name of station _Nester_

If it be a village, state the number of inhabitants.—_Ans._ _No village_

Also, the population to be supplied by the proposed office.—_Ans._ _About 200_

A diagram, or sketch from a map, showing the position of the proposed new office, with neighboring river or creek, roads and other post offices, towns, or villages near it, will be useful, and is therefore desired.

A correct map of the locality might be furnished by the county surveyor, but this must be without expense to the Department.

ALL WHICH I CERTIFY to be correct and true, according to the best of my knowledge and belief, this _Eighth_ day of _May_ 1891.

(☞ Sign full name.) _William Finley_ Proposed P. M.

I CERTIFY that I have examined the foregoing statement, and that it is correct and true, to the best of my knowledge and belief.

Fred L. Tuppard

Postmaster of _Mary Seth_

Clare co. Mich

(OVER.)

Be careful to answer the inquiries fully and accurately, or the case will not be acted upon.

This application was originally for a post office to be named Nester. As seen on the application, Nester was struck out and the name Nolan was added.

National Archives, Records Group 28: Records of the Post Office Department,1773-1950, Series: Report of Site Locations, 1837-1950, File Unit: Michigan: Ontonagon-Roscommon, p. 1011.

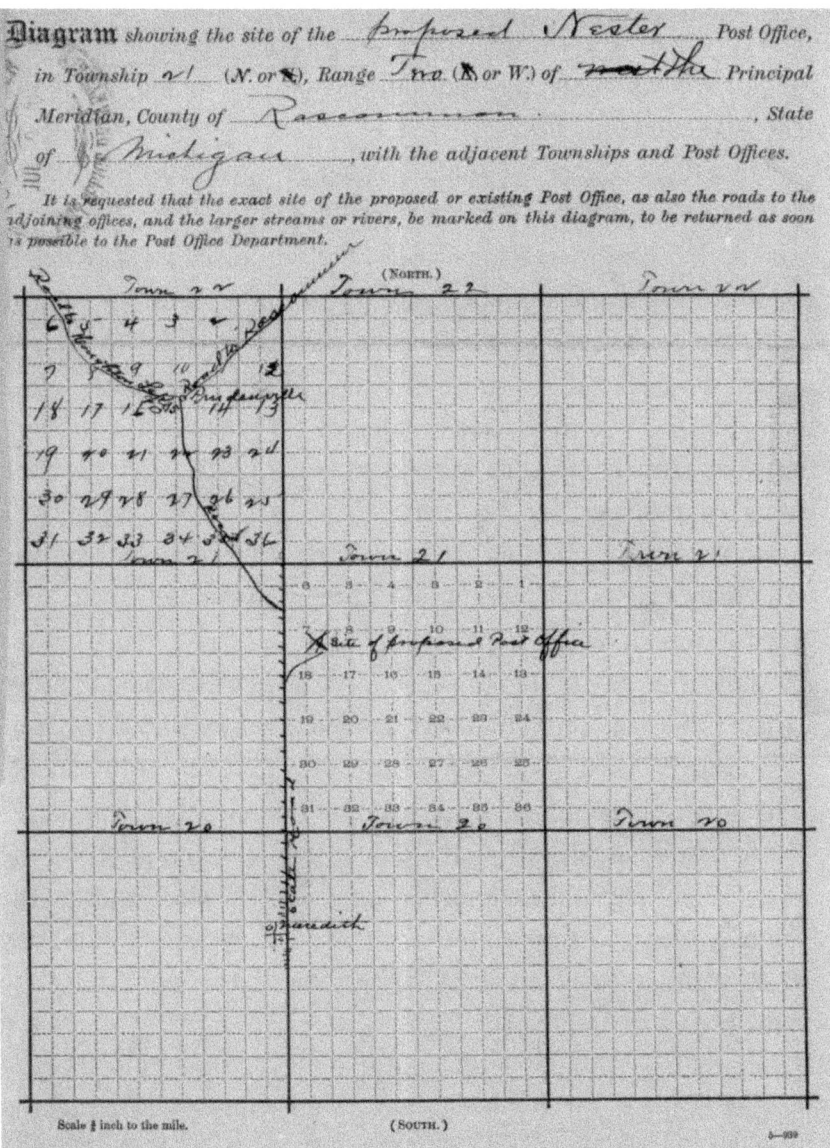

Diagram *showing the site of the* ~~proposed~~ *Nester* *Post Office,*
in Township 21 *(N. or S.), Range* Two. *(E. or W.) of* ~~north the~~ *Principal*
Meridian, County of Roscommon *, State*
of Michigan *, with the adjacent Townships and Post Offices.*

It is requested that the exact site of the proposed or existing Post Office, as also the roads to the adjoining offices, and the larger streams or rivers, be marked on this diagram, to be returned as soon as possible to the Post Office Department.

(NORTH.)

Scale ⅜ inch to the mile.   (SOUTH.)

This map shows the proposed location of the new post office of Nolan in section 7 of West Nester Township. It also shows its relationship to Prudenville, Meredith and the state road.

unsavory notoriety to the township and county, which, according to the *Roscommon News*, left "a stigma upon Roscommon county that it will take time to efface."[4]

The officials were accused of issuing forged orders (a written direction to pay money) and personally profiting from the deception. At the trial in February 1896, the witnesses presented "the chain of evidence and pictured to the jury how in the summer of 1893, the conspiracy originated, the issuing of large amounts of orders, the disposal of them by barter and sale, the destroying of the books and records by the burning of the schoolhouse and how the defendants in the case were identified with the fraud by their signatures to the orders in evidence."[5]

Ex-Supervisor Huntley* and ex-Clerk Robinson received two years in Ionia, and ex-Commissioner of Highways McDonald "was given 15 months at the same institution."[6]

At the trial, $17,000 in township orders were produced to prove an over issue had occurred. It was claimed that $80–90,000 in orders were issued. "Most of the orders were drawn in favor of members of the township board and disposed of at ridiculously low price."[7]

It is not clear if the township ever had to make good on the orders. According to the *Gladwin County Record*, since "most of the land in Nester township is pine woods, owned by Saginaw and Bay City lumbermen, they would have to pay the taxes should collection on the orders be enforced."[8]

Interestingly, there is no mention of William Finley being charged in the fraud case, even though his name appeared on the fraudulent orders. Furthermore, and similarly curious, Finley was arrested during this same timeframe for stealing "two yoke of oxen from Briggs & Cooper of Nester. The hides and heads of the oxen were found at Alpena, having been sold to a butcher at that place."

---

*   Huntley Lake is believed to have been named after Supervisor Huntley.

Finley had been a fugitive for four months prior to his arrest in December of 1895.[9] [10]

The worthless orders had "been handled and circulated in almost every city and hamlet in Michigan." Additionally, they had also been spread across neighboring states.[11]

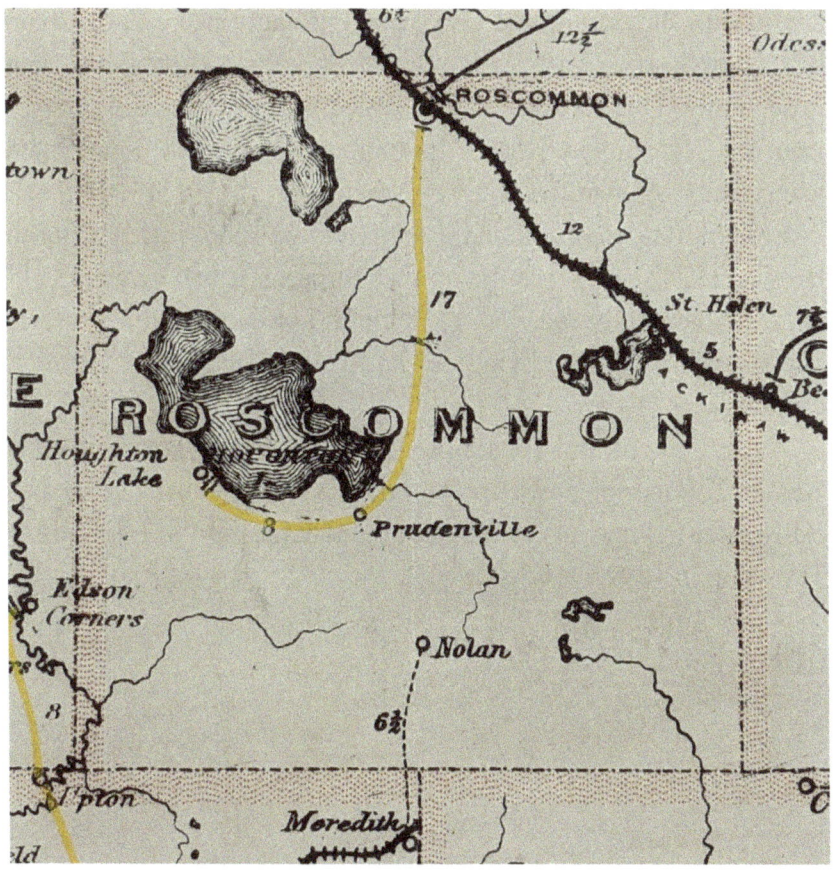

United States Post Office Dept. "Post route map of the states of Michigan and Wisconsin with adjacent parts of Ohio, Indiana, Illinois, Iowa and Minnesota showing post offices with the intermediate distances and mail routes in operation on the 1st. of October 1891." Map. Washington, D.C.: Post Office Dept., 1891.

Norman B. Leventhal Map & Education Center.

• • • • •

After the fraud case, little news came from "Old" Nolan. There were, over the years, references to short-lived mills in operation, cutting hardwoods, hemlock and swamp conifers.

John Davis (1844–1911), a well-noted resident of the area, operated one of these mills. He also owned property just east of Nolan in section 9. The Davis switch of the Hauptman Branch was also in section 9. This section was not owned by either the Roscommon Lumber Company or Nester. Its lumber was probably harvested using the Hauptman Branch.[12]

School classes continued even after the school arson. Sarah Brown (1874–1965) was the teacher for at least two years, 1894–95. She eventually married in 1896, ending her teaching career; she stayed in the Gladwin area and was buried in the Butman Cemetery.[13] [14]

As settlement and economic activity began to center in East Nester Township, news from "Old" Nolan diminished, especially after the post office moved to a new location in East Nester Township in 1899.

CHAPTER 17

The Actress, the General, and the Lawyer

She made her first appearance on the stage in April of 1886 in *Lily of Yeddo* at the Criterion Theatre in Brooklyn. Her stage name was Jane Stuart and she was not yet 16 years old. Her formal New York debut was made October 24, 1887, at the Fourteenth Street Theatre, as Ernestine in *Baron Rudolf*. Eventually, she joined the Crane's company at Decatur, Illinois, in September of 1889, playing such roles as Sallie Harmony in *On Probation*. She last worked playing a leading role in the company of Richard Mansfield.[1]

Miss Stuart received some acclaim during her short career on the stage. When she left the stage permanently in 1895, according to the *New York Times*, "her ability as an actress was best demonstrated in 'The Senator', in which she made a great hit. She was considered one of the most promising members of William H. Crane's company." Her real name was Jane S. Holahan, and together with her husband and his partner, she held title to the majority of West Nester Township beginning in 1903.[2]

Her husband was General Louis Auer of Milwaukee. He had seen her perform with Mr. Crane's company in Milwaukee and was so enamored that he followed her East and obtained an introduction. He successfully pressed his suit, and, on February 26, 1895, they were married, occasioning her to leave the stage permanently. It was one of the most interesting weddings of the day. President Cleveland, Secretary of War Lamont and Senator Murphy of New York sent letters of congratulations. It was attended by prominent political and business leaders, as well as by representatives of the medical, legal, and theatrical professions.

General Louis Auer (1857–1910)

The general was born in 1857 in Milwaukee. He gained his military title through his service with the Wisconsin National Guard. Over the years he rose in the ranks until Governor George W. Peck appointed him to the position of quartermaster general of the Wisconsin National Guard, a position he held until 1895. The elder Louis Auer (the general's father) came to Milwaukee in 1846 and formed a business that handled European passage, foreign exchange, and insurance. The young Auer joined the business in 1877 under the name Louis Auer & Son. After his father's death, he came to be recognized as the foremost real estate dealer in Milwaukee. "He negotiated many important realty transfers and he became prominently known as a speculative builder, erecting some of the finest structures in the city." He was also recognized for his civic-minded spirit and devotion to his community. The general died on February 15, 1910.[3]

Nathaniel Sawtelle Robinson (1867–1940)

While a student at the University of
Wisconsin

The general's partner in the Roscommon purchase was Nathaniel Sawtelle Robinson (1867–1940). Nathaniel received his law degree from the University of Wisconsin in 1890 and practiced law in Milwaukee his whole career. Sometime prior to 1903, he became acquainted with General Louis Auer and together they invested in

By 1904, Nathaniel Robinson and Louis Auer held title to the above parcels in West Nester Township. That year they sold a one-half interest in these parcels to Arthur E. Thomas and his brother Wesley M. Thomas. The parcels became the initial holdings of the Central Michigan Land Company, which the four partners formed that same year.

tax-reverted lands in Michigan. It is not known how these two partners became interested in investing in real estate together. Neither
is it understood how they may have learned of the tax lands that
John Carter had for sale in Roscommon County. Regardless, it is
their purchase that would shape the peculiar future of West Nester
Township after the original lumbermen were finished harvesting the
choice timber.

CHAPTER 18

The Central Michigan Land Company

On September 29, 1904, the Central Michigan Land Company, a Wisconsin corporation located in Milwaukee, purchased most of West Nester Township. Just the day before, Arthur E. Thomas and his brother Wesley M. Thomas, both from Chicago, had purchased an undivided one-half interest in this same parcel from Nathaniel S. Robinson and Susan N. Robinson, his wife, and from Louis Auer and Jane Stuart Auer, all from Milwaukee. Now the partners held this land as a corporate asset.

Previously, during July of 1903, the Milwaukee partners had bought tax lands amounting to 20,000-plus acres in township 21 N., range 2 W. (West Nester) for approximately $20,000. At that time, they were "offering to buy up all original titles on the lands when the price is reasonable. For the tax lands they do not own the original title, they propose to serve the statutory notice on the owners and make their title perfect."[1]

The purchase of these tax lands was part of the 125,000-plus acres that John Carter acquired in Roscommon County in 1902. It was from John Carter that Auer and Robinson had made their purchase in 1903.

By 1905, Carter's St. Helen Development Company was aggres-
sively promoting these lands. Their ad from March 1905 pro-
claimed: "Only a few years ago North Central Michigan was one
vast lumbering camp. The slaughter of the giant pines, however,
was but the first step in preparing the way for the development of
an agricultural region, rich in promise, and possessing all the conditions favorable to successful farming — virgin soils of great pro-
ductiveness, nearness to the unlimited markets of Chicago, Detroit
and other cities of the east, and transportation facilities the best that
could be desired." The Development Company touted these lands
by citing recent purchases as support to their claims: "The land is
extraordinarily well adapted to the growing of fruit, which is evi-
denced by the fact that we have sold to one orchard company a tract
of 20,000 acres, and to another 25,000 acres, all of which will be
planted to orchards and sold at not less than $150.00 per acre when
so planted." The tract of 20,000 acres is the parcel that ultimately
formed the Central Michigan Land Company holding.[2]

Officers and, undoubtedly, stockholders of the Central Michigan
Land Company changed over time. The Thomas brothers, however,
certainly dominated the list. Land transfer documents reveal that
Wesley M. Thomas was secretary in 1906, 1911 and 1912, Arthur
E. Thomas was vice-president in 1911, Clarence G. Thomas was
president in 1911 and 1912 and Charles B. Eggleston was vice-president in 1906.

From the few references available, it is difficult to glean the exact
intentions of the officers of the Central Michigan Land Company for
this property. Over time intentions may have changed. In September
of 1903, it was reported that the Milwaukee investors planned to
start a colony of Wisconsin farmers. Later, Colby Thomas related
that his relatives in Missouri "had 1100 acres of apple trees. Their
experience had been that about three of every eight years these trees
produced good crops, but lean years and good years taken together
the average annual net profit from this 1100 acre orchard was over

$12,200, a very nice income." Certainly, a large orchard was viewed as a viable possibility.[3]

Over time, the Central Michigan Land Company would sell several parcels of land from the original holdings and add others. Comparing the original Central Michigan Land Company purchase (1904, p. 110) to the Eggleston lawsuit description (1913–4, p. 156), shows the parcels sold and the parcels purchased during this time period. While the company was consolidating some interior sections, certain larger peripheral parcels were sold. Some of these transactions would be involved in the eventual legal proceedings between the company and Charles B. Eggleston.

CHAPTER 19

The Commission Merchant

B orn in Cincinnati in 1849, Charles Brier Eggleston was the only child of a successful commission merchant. His father "freighted goods from New Orleans and intermediate points, by steamboat to Cincinnati, by canal to Toledo, by lake to Buffalo, and by the Erie Canal and Hudson River to New York. He owned a line of canal boats, and did a very large and successful commission and forwarding business for many years." The son eventually followed a similar interest in business, and at twenty, he was a bookkeeper in his hometown. He moved to Chicago as a newlywed in 1871 (the year of the great fire) and remained a partner with his father in the firm of D. Eggleston & Son until 1877, the year his father died. This firm was eventually renamed C. B. Eggleston & Co and dealt in stocks, grain, and provisions.[1]

Charles, who everyone at the Chicago Board of Trade knew as "Sandy," was "an old member of the Board," and for years "a prominent operator." Eggleston's "specialty was carrying of property. He was one of the heaviest carriers on the board. He acted also as a sort of clearinghouse for numerous small traders."[2]

Though considered "one of the largest grain carriers in the country" and "at one time reputed to be the biggest cash grain dealer in the middle west," Charles was twice embroiled in failed market corners.[3] [4]

The first of these financial imbroglios occurred in 1887 and involved the collapse of the "Harper" corner on wheat. The collapse, which began on June 14, precipitated the failure of several Chicago firms and the suspension of others. One of the prominent firms behind the scenes was C. J. Kershaw & Co. Eggleston was "one of

Charles Brier Eggleston (1849–1919)

the leading figures in the Kershaw failure that resulted from the collapse of the Harper 'corner.'" Eggleston "lost $864,000 cash trying to save $25,000 special partnership interest in the Kershaw concern. He had some money left, however, and a wife worth $1,500,000."[5]

Over the next six years, Eggleston was "supposed to have made back nearly all he lost through Kershaw and Harper." But in 1893, he would be swept up in yet another "corner," this time involving lard and mess pork, the latter of which was barreled salt pork made up of shoulder and side meat. The collapse of this corner occurred on August 1, 1893, when "lard fell from $9.75 to $5.90 [in] a triece [sic] and pork from $18.75 to $10.50 a barrel." This occurred all in one day after months of speculation and manipulation.[6][7]

The night of the collapse, Eggleston "was busy at the office until midnight" and "he telegraphed in every direction for money. He spent an hour in a booth in the Long Distance Telephone office talking with people in other cities trying to arrange for funds to tide over the crisis. Money did not come" and "his failure followed." "Estimates around the board put Eggleston's losses at approximately $750,000. But the estimates were mere guesses." Charles, however, would once again recover from this severe business reversal.[8]

Charles was widely involved in other businesses and professional organizations. In 1883, he was elected vice-president of the National Elevator and Dock Company. At the same time, he held his membership in the Chicago Board of Trade and was a director of the Chicago Stock Exchange.

His business interests also included real estate. In 1889, he was partnered with James P. Mallette and Ralph E. Brownell. The firm of Eggleston, Brownell & Mallette, "constituted one of the leading real estate houses of the city." In 1894, two of their noteworthy developments were Eggleston and Auburn Park subdivisions, the "finest improved suburban property on the south side." This property extends from "Seventy-first Street to Seventy-ninth Street and is bounded on the east by State Street and the west by Wallace Street, being a mile long by three-fourth of a mile wide." Hundreds of homes were built there and on other south side sites, ranging in cost from $3,500 to $18,000. South Eggleston Avenue, cutting north and south through this development on the south side of Chicago, still carries his name today.[9]

The firm also owned the "large stone quarries at Thornton Il., which were opened in 1885 and from which they had taken the material for many of the beautiful drives and streets for which the south part of the city is famous." The construction department had "a most complete outfit of steam and horse rollers and other machinery for making roads" and during the season they gave "employment regularly to from 400 to 500 men." In Chicago, being "among the largest contractors of public improvement," they were contractors for "sewers, water mains, etc., and macadam streets, drives and boulevards." Though a full partner in this firm, Eggleston focused his "attention more particularly to other interests."[10]

Charles was married twice. His first marriage was to Maggie B. Wade in Cincinnati on May 8, 1871. They had one child, a son, Charles Evarts, born around 1874. Young Charles would be Eggleston's sole, and profligate, heir apparent. His father described him at 22 years of age as having "nearly ruined himself with whiskey and cigarettes" when during a scuffle in front of the family residence, the son, sodden with alcohol, threatened his father's life. Though Charles Sr. at first swore out a warrant, he relented, explaining that he was "anxious to place him in a sanitarium to restore his health." About a year prior, a less mild reformation was attempted by sending the reprobate son "against his will on a European tour in hope of weaning him from his Chicago associates and his ruinous habits." The father "had gratified the son's every whim and had given him all the advantages that wealth could confer." Nonetheless, all efforts by the parents failed to forestall young Charles's death at the age of 23 from "the effects of a [sic] overdose of morphine" in St. Louis, Missouri, on March 10, 1897.[11] [12]

Charles lost his first wife, Maggie, on January 12, 1906. He married his second wife, Mary, in Chicago on June 24, 1907. He was described at this time as being of average height, having a full beard, thinning gray hair and blue eyes set in an oval face with a high forehead. Charles and Mary had a childless marriage, leaving no direct heirs to two generations of business wealth.

CHAPTER 20

The Brothers Thomas

E dwin and Cornelia Thomas of Waukesha County, Wisconsin, had seven children, John Wix, Mary Isadore, Arthur Edwin, Clarence Gaius, Wesley Munger, Colby Nelson, and Albert Allison, all born in Wisconsin. Mary passed away in 1890, not yet 30 years old; the boys, on the other hand, all lived into their 70s and 80s, or, in the case of Albert, their 90s. All were sons of the American Revolution and could trace the Thomas lineage to William Thomas (1744–1789) of Massachusetts, a "Letter of Marque" captain.

Notwithstanding their agricultural background, several of the sons were able to garner both college and medical degrees. John, Arthur, and Wesley graduated from the University of Wisconsin in 1879, 1887, and 1892, respectively, with bachelor's degrees in science. Similarly, all three continued their education and received medical degrees from the Chicago Homeopathic Medical College in 1891, 1892 and 1895, respectively.

Of all the brothers, Dr. Arthur E. Thomas was most directly involved with the affairs of the Central Michigan Land Company, which he helped manage while also pursuing his medical practice. Following graduation, Arthur was a lecturer on Microscopy and Bacteriology at his alma mater from 1892–95. During 1897 he was lecturing on Physical Diagnosis and was a consulting physician at Chicago Baptist Hospital. Arthur also published medical case studies on such topics as gastric ulcers, mitral stenosis, and lead poisoning.

By 1901, his office, which he shared with his brother, Dr. Wesley M. Thomas, was located in the Reliance Building at 100 State Street (today 32 North State Street). It was described as "The Handsomest Suite of Physicians' Offices in the World."[1]

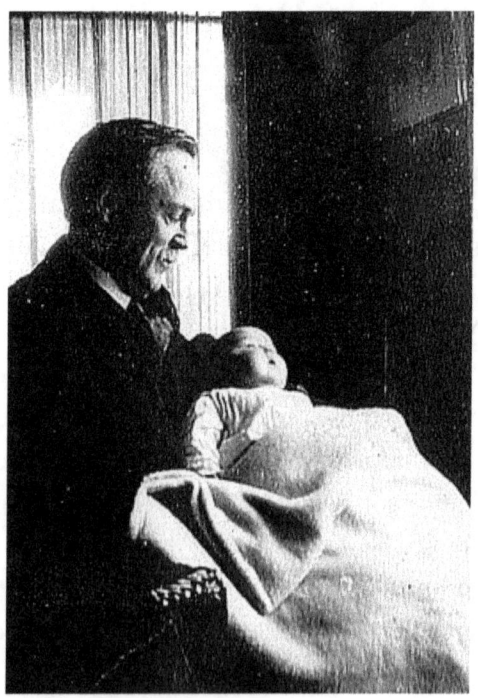

Arthur E. Thomas (1867–1937)

From the Thomas Family collection

The building was "famous as being the office headquarters of a greater number of physicians than any other building in Chicago," possibly the world. Two hundred physicians occupied the building.[2]

The office of Dr. Arthur E. Thomas, Associate Professor of Theory and Practice Medicine and Clinical Medicine in the Chicago Homeopathic Medical College, faced onto State Street. The office was fully equipped to examine and treat patients and had "a full and very complete set of electrical apparatus." Sharing this office was his brother Dr. Wesley M. Thomas, Adjunct Professor of Medicine and Lecturer on Clinical Diagnosis in the Chicago Homeopathic Medical College. He had "an established business in the examination of pathological specimens and fluids, in blood-analysis, and examination of stomach contents."[3]

Arthur resided on Indiana Avenue in Chicago, at several different residences from 1895 to 1910. During this same period Charles Eggleston maintained his residence at 3336 Indiana Avenue. From 1898 to 1902, the two lived only about a block apart, in a neighborhood that was considered "high end" at the turn of the century. Since that time, the neighborhood (part of today's Bronzeville) has fallen on hard times and the grand homes have been razed.

The elder son, John Wix, was an attending Physician and Surgeon at Rockford City Hospital in Rockford, Illinois, in 1897. By 1900, he had settled in Arizona where he would remain the rest of his life. He was active in the Arizona State Board of Medical Examiners and held the position of secretary for a number of years.

Soon after John relocated to Arizona, the brothers became involved in another business pursuit that just preceded their involvement with the Central Michigan Land Company. Apparently not averse to investing in disparate business ventures, the brothers, with other investors, organized the Nogales Copper Company in Arizona in 1902, which held mineral lands in Arizona and Mexico. $3,000,000 was raised to capitalize this venture. The company office was located at 1018 Tribune Building in Chicago while the mine office was in Nogales, Santa Cruz County, Arizona. One hundred men were employed in 1904. Three of the brothers were officers, Arthur was president, Wesley was secretary and Colby was general manager.

The next son, Clarence Gaius, was a farmer for most of his life. He was an officer of the Central Michigan Land Company and he also moved out to Arizona by 1920, joining John, Arthur, and Colby.

Before his move out west, Colby Nelson was a frequent visitor to the Central Michigan Land Company property and in 1910 he was referred to as the manager. As mentioned above, he was, in 1904, listed as the general manager of the Nogales Copper Company. By 1920 he was located in Arizona as a farmer.

The youngest brother, Albert Allison, spent two years (1891–92) of college preparatory studies at Hillsdale College in Michigan. Just two years later he returned to the family farm having married in 1894. Albert would be the first brother to live on and manage the Central Michigan Land company holdings.

Arthur, as mentioned, was the most intimately involved in the Central Michigan Land Company's property. It is difficult to explain his ardor, especially considering his medical career in Chicago. His firm resolution to find success from the Nester Township investment would ultimately drive him to forsake his medical career in Chicago and permanently reside on the property, beginning in about 1913.

Besides managing the property, Arthur was also active in township politics once he was a resident. This was perhaps a means to supplement his income. In 1914, he was a township commissioner. In 1915, contention over a recent election led to the courts settling a dispute between Arthur Thomas and Harold Morrison, both of whom were officers. During the election in 1916, an apparent altercation between Arthur Thomas and Charlie Winkler, another Nester resident, occurred that led to a criminal case. Arthur was charged with assault and battery but was found not guilty the following April.[4][5][6][7]

Arthur would stay on the property until the death of Charles Eggleston in 1919.

CHAPTER 21

Destructive Distillations

O f the various efforts by the Central Michigan Land
Company to profit from its investment in Nester Township,
the most remarkable was the production of turpentine.
Since much of its land had recently been clear cut and burned,
and now resembled a battlefield dotted with huge pine stumps, the
production of turpentine appeared a logical outlet for stumps that
would have to be removed regardless, if another potential project, a
fruit orchard, could begin. Undoubtedly, it was enticing to imagine
stump removal as a means to "open up an avenue of profit from
what had heretofore been a sheer expense to those clearing the
land."[1]

In 1907, just as the first experiments with turpentine production
began, it was "estimated the thousands of stumps which cover the
state are now worth, for the turpentine they contain, nearly as much
as the trees were thirty or forty years ago." This claim would be
viewed as outrageously hyperbolic in a mere seven years.[2]

The Central Michigan Land Company was not the first concern
to enter this type of business in northern Michigan. Coon (William
H.) & Leary operated a small turpentine plant in Roscommon.
It began operation during the summer of 1905 but burned to the
ground the following November. By January of 1906, William H.

Coon was assisting Dr. Arthur E. Thomas in designing the machinery and apparatus for the Central Michigan Land Company's plant.

CHARCOAL & TURPENTINE PLANT
THOMAS RANCH NOLAN MICH.

McKinnon Boiler & Machine Co. of Bay City received the contract to provide the equipment for this new plant and submitted their proposal on February 5, 1906. They planned to furnish "6 retorts 4 ft. 6 in. diameter, 20 ft. long." Each retort had a door on one end, an "8 in. diameter open top dome 10 in. high on each shell" and a trough on the bottom. Through the top opening would pass the distillate as it evaporated out of the stump pieces.[3]

Another important feature of these retorts was an "18 in. track gauge inside and full length of each retort." This track would allow for the cars carrying the pine to be moved in and out of the retorts. The cars were "19 ft. 10 in. long over all, each with five sets 7 in. diameter, 2 in. face truck wheels."[4]

McKinnon Boiler also supplied "6 coolers 4 ft. 6 in. diameter, 20 ft. long" with doors on one end. Like the retorts, the coolers had tracks for the cars running the length of the inside.[5]

It was in these retorts that the red pine stump pieces underwent the process of destructive distillation. As heat was applied to the sealed retorts, all the oils, resins and liquids would evaporate from the stump chips. The distillates would travel out the top of the retort. Eventually, all that would be left was charcoal. Apparently, some heavier substances would accumulate in a trough running along the bottom of the retort.

How exactly the distillate was condensed is unclear, but the assumption is that the coolers received these gases via piping from the top of the retort. Why the coolers had tracks running the length of the inside is also unclear.

Some idea of how the process worked by 1911 can be gleaned from reports of the Crown Chemical Company plant in Grayling. Here the "stumps are first pulled with a stump puller, then blasted apart and delivered to the factory." The retorts were "six feet in diameter and twenty feet long, set in brick, and with fire boxes underneath. When the retorts are filled the doors are sealed air-tight and the steam and heat then applied in such a manner and the turpentine oils are vaporized and pass through condensers to the receiving tank, while the tar and oils pass off from the retorts through other pipes to their respective tanks. The crude turpentine is then placed in stills and by certain processes and the application of heat and steam the volatile oils and foreign matter are separated from the turpentine, which comes through a system of condensers a pure water white, ready for the market. The crude tar is marketable as tar immediately upon coming from the retorts, but it is not sold as such, being much more valuable when worked up into by-products."[6]

By May the equipment was delivered by rail to the Central Michigan Land Company's site just southwest of Clear Lake.

Apparently, this first effort at producing turpentine was "on a small scale, largely in the line of an experiment." Though the plant was reported to be successful, the retorts were not gas-tight, resulting in a legal squabble between the contractor and the Central Michigan Land Company. Surprisingly, the case was eventually settled by the Michigan Supreme Court ruling of March 16, 1909. The Central Michigan Land Company had lost the jury trial for failing to make full payment, as well as payment for additional costs for certain extras not previously billed. The Supreme Court affirmed the lower court's ruling on all points.[7] [8]

It was also found "that the condensers which were made of copper, brazed at the joints, was not the ideal way of making a brazing solder and interfered with the manufacture of turpentine." To solve this problem, in "the new condensers, stills, and tanks, seamless copper of a thicker gauge" would be used.[9]

Regardless of the ongoing legal battle, in March of 1907, it was reported that "the company determined to enlarge operations and the old plant is being dismantled and one of double its capacity is to be erected, and the machinery is arriving on the ground. It is the intention to have the plant in operation early in the spring." The report went on to state that "the experimental plant had six retorts," while the new plant would "have twelve, thus doubling the capacity of the work."[10] [11]

The enlarged plant was inspected by the Michigan Department of Labor on September 21, 1907. Sixty-three male employees were noted producing the turpentine. The following year, and the last recorded inspection, seventy-nine male employees were found producing turpentine and lumber. In the fall of 1909, it was described as a "new up-to-date turpentine plant which has a capacity of 24 cords of stumps per day." About 50 men were employed.[12] [13] [14]

Red pine stumps were the preferred raw material for these northern turpentine plants because of their resinous nature. The main resulting product was known as wood turpentine or stump turp. Always quick to extol a new industry, the *Gladwin County Record* stated that "turpentine procured from Michigan norway (red pine) is superior in quality to the product of the southern pine, being less rank" and that "there is also produced a superior quality of norway pine tar, pine tar oil, a disinfectant warranted to destroy bedbugs, carpet beetles and all insects that infest residences, a fine article of embalming fluid, and sheep dip for killing ticks and curing scab on sheep."[15]

The process of extracting these products from the pine stumps was known as destructive distillation, a name that distinguished it from the process of distilling the pine resin obtained from tapping live pine trees, an operation process common in the southern states. At the Central Michigan Company's plant, this process was described as follows in 1910: "The stump is pulled; thoroughly cleaned of dirt, drawn to the factory, sawed into chunks by a circular saw, the chunks loaded into the retorts, thoroughly baked, until every particle of liquid is removed, and what is left is a good quality of charcoal, which is used for heating the next retort's filling of pine stumps." At this time, Thomas J. Kehoe was reported to have been in charge of work at the plant for the previous four years.[16]

Percy Briggs, who worked for the Central Michigan Land Company for several years in his late teens during the time the new plant was operating, described the stump removal efforts almost 70 years after his employment. "Every day a professional blaster, with dynamite, blew the stumps and split them up. They had a big 'Nicholas-Shepard' steam engine and used a large cable about 500 ft. long. They would connect the cable from the engine to the blasted stump and try to pull out the stump. That didn't last long. The stay bolts and rivets in the engine began to leak so badly they couldn't keep any steam in the boiler. [...] Then they went to the 3-legged stilyards and a team pulling out the stumps. The horses held the load until three men cleaned the dirt from the stumps." Recalling the turpentine plant operation, Percy related how they "set up those huge retorts, or tanks, there were six or seven of them, about 100 feet long and 8 feet across. Tracks, like a railroad, ran into the retorts. Six or eight little cars, holding about 1 ½ cords of stumps each, were pushed into the retort and the door closed. The other end was already bolted and sealed. A fire was built around the retorts and the turpentine was fried out. Also tar and charcoal were produced." Percy's memory is somewhat faulty, however, for the retorts were never reported to be 100 feet long.[17]

There is scant reference to the turpentine plant after 1909. In August of 1910, the plant was reported as being repaired and scheduled to run 3–4 months. During June of 1912, it was claimed that the firm would resume operations on a much larger scale than heretofore. The last mention in the local papers is from 1914, commenting that the plant was not operating of late. Like all the northern Michigan turpentine plants, the Central Michigan Land Company's plant was short lived. There is no evidence that any of these northern Michigan plants continued to operate past the start of World War I. Even the most enduring of these facilities, the Cadillac Turpentine Company, was last inspected in 1914. Apparently, stump turp could not compete with the more traditional product of southern pines.[18]
[19] [20]

It was not until February of 1919 that the turpentine plant, long inoperative, was finally dismantled and the "machinery, tanks, and boilers sent to a Bay City salvage."[21]

In the tall grass, southwest of Clear Lake, are the remains of this one example of a heralded new industry that was thought to be able to provide a profitable means to convert cutover lands into agricultural lands. There are the footings and foundation from the plant and the hidden remnants of pine tar, seemingly impervious to age. Adjacent to this site is a small phalanx of cephalopod-like stumps, long since uprooted, still waiting for their day to be processed.

CHAPTER 22

The Milwaukee Fruit Farm

Referred to locally as the Milwaukee Fruit Farm, the Milwaukee Peach Farm, the Thomas Ranch, the Roscommon County Fruit Farm, or just simply the Fruit Farm, the Central Michigan Land Company's holdings were confusingly polyonymous.

Though it owned the bulk of the township, the headquarters was located near the southwest shore of Clear Lake. During the early years of the company, the Hauptman Branch still ran to Nolan, which was located farther south in East Nester Township.

The operation itself was an anomaly in scale and locale. What was a large apple orchard doing surrounded by miles of cutover land in the hills of southern Roscommon County, especially far removed from other agricultural lands? The Central Michigan Land Company was seemingly an enterprise with unlimited capital to invest and an unrealistic optimism about the agricultural potential of the land. Though in the early stages, the future appeared promising to the investors in the Central Michigan Land Company, the cost of clearing the land, building a turpentine operation, constructing buildings, and employing up to 150 people would eventually tax even their sizeable capital resources, while the limited agricultural capacity of this land would inevitably reveal itself. Still, as late as

1912, it was reported that they had "unlimited capital behind the enterprise."[1]

The primary agricultural effort of the company was the orchard. Within a year of its formation, the company had "a good start on their orchard near Nolan. They have cleared 100 acres upon which they have planted 5,000 trees." The glowing reports of the suitability of this land as a fruit producer were championed in 1907 and the conversion from stump land to fruit trees was described thus: "the land was cleared and hundreds of fruit trees set out, it being demonstrated to be a fine fruit region."[2][3]

Once again Percy Briggs's recollection provides an invaluable first-person account of two initial years of the company's agricultural efforts, spanning 1906 and 1907. Percy first worked planting nursery stock about a mile west of F-97, an easily identifiable location today. He "set out thousands of small seedlings getting ready for the orchard." Later, he worked in the barn caring for the horses. He recalled that it "was a great place to work at the time" and that he was paid "$20 per month, with my board, too."[4]

In October of 1910 a writer for the Gladwin paper accompanied the Nester Township clerk on a tour of Nester Township. Reviewing the company's pomological efforts, the writer reported that "Four years ago the company set out 50,000 apple trees, covering 240 acres of the land from which the turpentine factory had consumed the stumps. The trees are very thrifty. When set out they were whips about two feet high, but have grown to good sized trees, some of which produced apples the present year." This noted density of trees per acre (208) was probably a little high for the era, though not unusual today. A year later, it was claimed that the orchard had "10,000 Jonathan, 1,000 Wealthy, also Duchess of Oldenburg. These trees are 6 years old and are bearing some this year." Arthur Thomas's plans were to "set out next spring 7,000 peach and 3,000 plum." If this was ever done, they did not survive, but it may explain why the farm was at times referred to as the Milwaukee Peach Farm.[5] [6]

The economic success of the orchard is questionable. On its own, it certainly was not capable of carrying all the expenses of the company, as is evident in the change of ownership. Nevertheless, the orchard continued to contribute economically to the enterprise as late as 1918. That year, Arthur Thomas purchased a new Ford truck to take a fine crop of apples to market.[7] [8]

Not all the land cleared of stumps was dedicated to the orchard. Where the slope was advantageous, small fields were cleared for crops. During the summer of 1910, crops were doing well and the fall harvest of rye, oats, and corn was excellent. Twenty acres of potatoes had also been planted. Like the orchard, these fields were worked year after year. Arthur Thomas purchased a tractor in the spring of 1917 to rush plowing and other farm work. It was successful enough that he was hauling grain to West Branch in December. Several years later the property foreman, Velma Entrekin, was seeking to hire a crew to husk corn. Though eventually these fields would provide hay only, as late as 1927 thrashing grain was a fall occupation.[9] [10] [11] [12] [13] [14]

Predictably, with such extensive land holdings and only a fraction devoted to the orchard and small crop fields, the raising of livestock was also attempted. The first endeavor was with sheep. In late 1911, 2,000 sheep were received and placed on the property. An extensive stock-rearing plan was promulgated. A year later, the same number of sheep were shipped to Chicago. Though the record is scant, sheep were still being brought to the Fruit Farm to be pastured as late as 1920.[15] [16] [17]

Cattle were also pastured on the property. Though again the record is meager, from 1919 through 1921 cattle were brought to the property during the spring and rounded up prior to the winter. In 1919, the cattle were taken to Gladwin in December after spending the season on the property. Two hundred head of Clement Township cattle were brought to the Fruit Farm in April and May of 1920. In October of 1921, cattle were being rounded up on the property, though 18 head were missing in late December.[18] [19] [20] [21] [22] [23]

CHAPTER 23

Social Milieu, Charivari, etc.

T he budding settlement on the Fruit Farm, as mentioned, had all the attributes of a small town with a noteworthy social life. Holidays, births, and marriages were significant occasions for this isolated community. Additionally, the company's mildly paternalistic policy included, among other things, a school-house as well as a preacher for Sunday services. All of this was most commonplace during the period 1905–10, the heady years of greatest company optimism.

Albert Thomas, the youngest of the Thomas brothers, was the first manager of the Central Michigan Land Company's property, from at least 1906 to early 1910.

With such a large crew of laborers living on the property it was inevitable that the first birth occurred summarily. Susie, the wife of Jessie C. Adelblue, the field boss at the time, gave birth to a baby girl they named Atta on September 13, 1907. Almost exactly a year later, on September 18, 1908, another girl, named Iva, was born to Orlie B. Ansted and wife Rosie B. (photo, p. 137).[1] [2]

Early in 1908, Orlie had moved his family to the Fruit Farm, having accepted a dual position of bookkeeper and preacher. Orlie had attended Hillsdale College (1902–05) and was ordained as an American Baptist Minister. Orlie evangelized at the schoolhouse but also held prayer meetings at private homes. His Sunday services were well attended and at times two services were held as well as a Sunday school. In April 1908, Easter services were held at Albert Thomas's (the Big House), the house being nicely decorated. Some young people from Butman attended and there were singing and socializing also on the agenda. Eventually, the Fruit Farm lost its preacher when Orlie and his family moved in late spring or early summer of 1910.[3] [4] [5] [6] [7] [8]

Infrequent religious gatherings persisted on the Fruit Farm. In June of 1921, the Gladwin paper reported that "the L.D.S. Sunday school picnic held at Verncroft was a decided success." The group, after an hour program, enjoyed swimming and fishing. "At the close a vote of thanks was given Velma Entrekin in appreciation of furnishing grove, tables and privilege of the lake."[9]

When Carl Raymond and his young wife, Vada, were feted at the Fruit Farm during late November 1907, fifty men and boys treated them to a charivari,* though apparently not as enforcement of any social standards but to simply celebrate their recent status as newlyweds. Undoubtedly, this would have included a mock serenade and the banging of pots and pans. Gifts were given and several neighbors spoke on their behalf followed by community singing.[10]

Holidays such as Independence Day, Thanksgiving, and Christmas were also celebrated. The company provided for the working families in small ways during the holidays. A large crowd gathered on the evening of the 4th of July, 1907, to enjoy fireworks. Later that year, turkeys were given to each family for Thanksgiving. In 1908, after the crew had been hunting in late December, the families gathered at Albert Thomas's for music, singing, recitations and games.[11] [12] [13]

The necessity of a school on the Fruit Farm grew with the population. By the fall of 1907, a schoolhouse was built, and a bell raised.

---

*   Or 'shivaree,' a noisy mock serenade to a newly married couple.

Orlie Burton Ansted (1877–1971) and wife, Rosie, with children Harold and Iva several years after leaving the Fruit Farm.

Besides normal instruction, the school was used for church service and social events for both the children and adults. In December 1907, the school children had a social at the schoolhouse and provided entertainment to the adults. The following May entertainment was again at the schoolhouse, celebrating bird and flower day.

In 1909–10 the schoolteacher was Miss Worges. Classes started around September 6, with time off for the Christmas holidays. As an indication of the remoteness of the Fruit Farm, Miss Marie Wiresley, the new teacher for 1910–11, was delayed returning to her duties in January 1911, hampered by impassable roads. School sessions were maintained intermittently until as late as 1919.[14][15][16][17]

CHAPTER 24

Buildings

When the Central Michigan Land Company began developing its lands in West Nester Township, it centered its activity on the south shore of Clear Lake. There, the Wright Lumber Company had abandoned its camp and rail network by 1897. When the Central Michigan Land Company began to advance its plans there, building construction would be one of its first concerns.

The company first utilized a large building at the lake that had housed locomotive engines. The building measured 50' x 150' and was eventually converted into a bunkhouse. Inside, two "men slept in a bunk, there was one wash stand, about 8 feet long, and two barrels of water so you could wash the sand out of your hair. No hot water, but there was drinking water pumped from the lake," per Percy W. Briggs's account from memories of his work there during two early seasons with the company.[1]

By 1907 the company had built a store, cook building, a bunkhouse and horse barn. There was also a sawmill next to the turpentine plant.

At the store, farm goods were bought and shipped out for sale on the train. In its time, this store was "good for the people of the surrounding country, as you could sell any produce you could raise."

COMPANY STORE

COMPANY STORE THOMAS RANCH NOLAN MICH.

LAWRENCE ELBERT ON BARK STORAGE PILE

TYPICAL WORKERS HOUSE ON THOMAS RANCH
LAWRENCE ELBERT & MABEL THOMAS
AT RIGHT

The Thomas Ranch was one of several local names for the Central
Michigan Land Company's property.

Similarly, lumber manufactured at the sawmill was also shipped out for sale. Remnant pine, hemlock, birch, maple, ash and oak were harvested. It was at the sawmill that the stumps were also cut up for processing in the turpentine factory.[2]

Another forest product harvested by the company was hemlock bark. Hemlock lumber was inferior to white pine for building purposes and was bypassed by the early lumbermen. For this reason, much hemlock had been left standing on the lands purchased by the Central Michigan Land Company. The bark was peeled from newly harvested trees and air dried. It was then shipped to tanneries where it played a crucial role in the tanning process because of the bark's high tannin content (photo, "Lawrence Elbert on Bark Storage Pile," p. 141).

Individual housing was also provided for some company workers. There were at least ten of these housing units along the main road, west of the headquarters building. These were framed buildings covered with what appears to be tar paper (photo, "Typical Workers House on Thomas Ranch," p. 141).

The Big House (headquarters), where the Company manager lived, was constructed in 1907. In October of that year, it was reported that the "new cement house of A. A. Thomas is going up fast and will be a two-story house made of cement blocks." It is possible that reference to cement blocks may imply that the blocks were made on site with a hand-tamp block machine. This saved the cost of transportation and eliminated the loss from breakage. Cement and aggregate were hand mixed, then poured into the mold. Hundreds of blocks could be turned out in a day (photo, p. 143).[3]

This house would be the signature building for the Central Michigan Land Company. Located southwest of the lake on the high ground that rimmed its shore, it would reflect the commitment the company was making to its investment in West Nester. It went on to house a succession of managers and owners and it continues to endure, long past the time that recollections of the company and its principals have faded from the land.

Central Michigan Land Company headquarters
building, constructed in 1907.

CHAPTER 25

Some Unpolished Verse

V ery few first-person accounts exist of West Nester. Yet, by way of a poem, we are furnished with a tale of a brief visit during the winter of 1907–08. It is a short accounting of people, topography, and buildings. Though the account takes place in the winter, there are a surprising number of people mentioned. The author also comments that dwellings were quite plentiful and mentions a boarding house, bunkhouse, store, stables, and a house by the lake. The fruit farm is described as prosperous and charming.

Roscommon Co. Fruit Farm

J. M. R. - G. T. P.

I was some where the other day
 They called it the fruit farm
& every thing looked prosperous there
 To me it was a charm

I Saw Sweet Ernie in the valley
 & Vada On the hill
& for to go back there some time
I declare I think I will

We got good Grub at the boarding house
 Where we did stop at noon
The table & the benches long
 Just gave us lots of room

They told me of the Bunking house
 & plent(y) they wer their*
It made me stear for an other place
 & that I do declare

I saw my friends wer plenty
 As I went Snooping round
I could not see the Soil a bit
 For the snow up on the ground

I went in the Lovely store
 & it was nice & long
The friends & strangers that wer there
 They looked at Uncle John

Then I went unto the Barn
 It was all'Stables there
The Boss he was a Gentle man
 & that I do declare

---

* The irregular and/or incorrect spelling in the verse is as it appears in the
 original.

I led my horse down to the lake
 Neighbor Johny was a head
He had a lodgeing place for me
 My Supper & the bed

The dwellings wer quite plenty to
 When I cast my eye around
& between them lovely mountains
 The fruit farm there I found

When I got redy to go away
 The wind was blowing raw
She said good by Mr. Reynolds
 It was my sweet sister in law[1]

CHAPTER 26

Badger, Verncroft, and the Riddle of Jacwac

By 1909, activity at the Fruit Farm had required the settling of many families and single laborers on the property. There was land being cleared for the orchard as well as several farm fields. Employment was also available at the turpentine plant and sawmill. For a brief period, this development was optimistically referred to as the new town of Badger by the Gladwin paper in and around September 1909. It was a name that was not, perhaps, surprising, as most of the original investors were from Wisconsin. Some, including Nathaniel Robinson, Wesley Thomas, and Arthur E. Thomas, were graduates of the University of Wisconsin, Badgers all. This appellation never stuck, though others would.[1]

With the closing of the Nolan post office in the southern part of the township on July 30, 1909, and the growing settlement at the Fruit Farm, there was an increased urgency for postal service in this part of the county. After the Nolan post office closed, Butman in Gladwin County was then the nearest post office to Nester Township. Jacwac was the unusual name given to the post office established on the Fruit Farm to alleviate this deficiency. This short-lived post office was opened on December 18, 1909. Not surprisingly, the first postmaster was Albert A. Thomas, the Central Michigan Land Company manager. Supplies for this new post office did not arrive until April of 1910. And though it was reported closed by May 31, 1910, on October 22 a civil service exam was scheduled at Butman to fill a contemplated postmaster position at Jacwac. No record exists that it ever reopened.[2][3][4]

The name Jacwac is such a discordant and contrived name for a post office that it draws attention to its etymology. Given the influence of the Thomas brothers at the Fruit Farm and the fact that one of them would be the first postmaster, it can be only explained in one fashion. It is a simple acronym for the brothers that perfectly match their names and almost the order of birth: John, Arthur, Clarence, Wesley, Albert, and Colby.

A second attempt at establishing a post office at the Fruit Farm was more enduring and began September 26, 1914, when Carrie C. Thomas became the first postmaster of Verncroft. Carrie was the wife of Arthur E. Thomas who was now managing the property for Charles Eggleston. Mail was handled here until April 15, 1921. The settlement at the Fruit Farm would bear this name a few years past the closing of the post office, until at least 1923. An early plat book from the late 1930s still located Verncroft near Clear Lake.[5][6][7][8]

CHAPTER 27

Taking Up the Last Steel

I t had begun in the fall of 1877 in the wake of the Gerrish & Hazelton Railroad's success in Clare County the year before. Industrial logging, utilizing trains for transportation, arrived in West Nester Township, as the first rails were placed en route to Lake Thomas. This orgy of biomass extraction would end in a mere thirty-some years, until the Hauptman Branch was finally taken up.

As early as 1899, as the Boyce timber was playing out, the Michigan Central began taking out some of the sidetracks and switches along the western end of the Hauptman Branch. One indication that the Boyce Lines were retreating and becoming less important was in June of that year. That month the phone lines running the length of the Hauptman Branch and facilitating the railroad company's management of the line were adjusted such that the phone box was moved to the Y. Yet, it wasn't until 1905 that it was first announced that the whole line was vulnerable. The truth underlying this speculation would be delayed until 1907, when seemingly contrary news was reported that the line had been taken up in the Boyce timber but might be advanced to Houghton Lake. This proposed extension was to service the Michelson development at the upper reaches of the Muskegon River, a task that the Grand Rapids & Indiana Railway would ultimately undertake. The extension of the Hauptman Branch to Houghton Lake struck a familiar chord though. Similar to when the citizens of Prudenville had hoped for the re-railing of the old Roscommon Lumber Company line, having a rail connection was still the aspiration of the citizens along the lake.[1] [2] [3] [4]

Unfortunately for those living along the south shore of Houghton Lake, it was only speculation that the line would be preserved. Though there was still lumbering activity along the Hauptman for several more years, particularly at Nolan in East Nester Township, it would prove to be insufficient to retain the line for long. The Coan mill at Nolan still operated until 1908 but with a diminishing output. This slow decline of activity at Nolan resulted in the post office being discontinued by August of 1909.[5] [6]

A year after the collapse of Nolan, the Gladwin paper stated that the branch was being taken up. This was the remaining main line and spur running to Nolan. By the fall of 1910, both the Gladwin paper and the Roscommon paper noted that the nearest railroad to Nester Township was now St. Helen. The age of rail was over for Nester Township.[7] [8] [9]

The loss of the Hauptman Branch caused transportation difficulties in Nester Township. This was especially true for the Central Michigan Land Company. In 1912, the Thomas brothers were working with West Branch businessmen in "the opening and improving of the old Hauptman railroad bed leading from their ranch and turpentine plant into West Branch." Today, public use of the old railroad bed as a seasonal road through East Nester Township is a result of that need for access and the efforts of citizens such as the Thomas brothers.[10]

CHAPTER 28

1910 Census and Constraints

It is difficult to distinguish which households in the 1910 (April) census for Nester Township are located in the western half. Fortunately, several factors help distinguish some of these households. Most obviously, eleven households have occupants specifically identified as employed at the fruit farm and all but one note that they are renting their homes, an assumed arrangement on company property. Additionally, little land was available outside the company property in West Nester Township. Also, though Nolan had just lost its rail connection and the Coan Lumber Company had recently ended operations, most settlement in the township was still centered in East Nester Township.[1]

Fifty-four people, 33 of whom are children, occupy the eleven households on the fruit farm. The occupations for the head of households include 3 laborers, 2 teamsters, a horseman, a carpenter, a farmer, a foreman, a washer-woman and a clergyman/bookkeeper.

The clergyman/bookkeeper was Orlie Ansted and the foreman was Thomas Kehoe. There were still enough children to justify a school and the teacher was Mabel Christie.

Elsewhere in West Nester Township, E. M. Hiestand of Chicago was developing section 30 for agriculture. He was one of few individuals to buy land from the Central Michigan Land Company. The supervisor of Sherman Township, G. C. Brown, had just the past fall planted 10 acres of wheat and 70 acres of rye on the portion of the property that was plains and free of timber.[2]

Though the Central Michigan Land Company had commenced its management of the West Nester property with noteworthy avidity, by 1910, a variety of changes must have been tempering this enthusiasm. Turpentine production had ended and though there would be talk of reviving the plant for a few more years, it would prove to be uneconomical. Substantial land sales were not materializing. Additionally, key employees were turning over. Orlie Ansted left the company's employ in 1910 and his bookkeeper duties were taken up by Caroll Thomas, Arthur's 20-year-old son. Albert Thomas also vacated his position as manager and returned to Milwaukee.

Other changes affecting the company included the loss of the Hauptman Branch, which exacerbated transportation issues. Money concerns had required that the company go into debt since 1908 simply to continue operations. This debt would grow over the coming years. Moreover, if he still held an interest in the company, surely the passing of General Louis Auer (one of the founding investors) in February of 1910, would have adversely affected the resources of the company. This would be especially true if his widow refused additional subsidies and/or sought to sell her interest. All of this was a prelude to the grim days ahead for the company. Nonetheless, the company was still actively farming the property and maintaining the buildings.[3] [4] [5]

CHAPTER 29

Charles B. Eggleston vs. the Central Michigan Land Co.

T hough Charles Eggleston was not one of the founding owners of the Central Michigan Land Company (1903–04), his
involvement began near the start. As noted earlier, land
records have him as vice-president in 1906. However, as a friend
and neighbor of Arthur E. Thomas in Chicago, it is easy to believe
that he invested soon after the company's formation.

Over time, the company became increasingly indebted to
Eggleston. On Monday, May 11, 1908, at 2:00 p.m., the company
officers met in room 615 of the First National Bank in Chicago and
accepted a loan of $15,000 from Arthur E. Thomas. Thomas hoped
to obtain a mortgage on the property until some company lumber
could be sold. At a following meeting in Milwaukee on October 17
at 2:10 p.m., the company issued a note to Thomas secured by a
mortgage on the Roscommon property. Two days later Thomas sold
the mortgage to Eggleston.[1]

Apparently, Eggleston was eager to accumulate the company's
debt. In April of 1911, Eggleston also paid the company $3,000
to pay off an additional debt owed to Thomas. The next year, the
company secured another mortgage for $13,341.24 from Eggleston

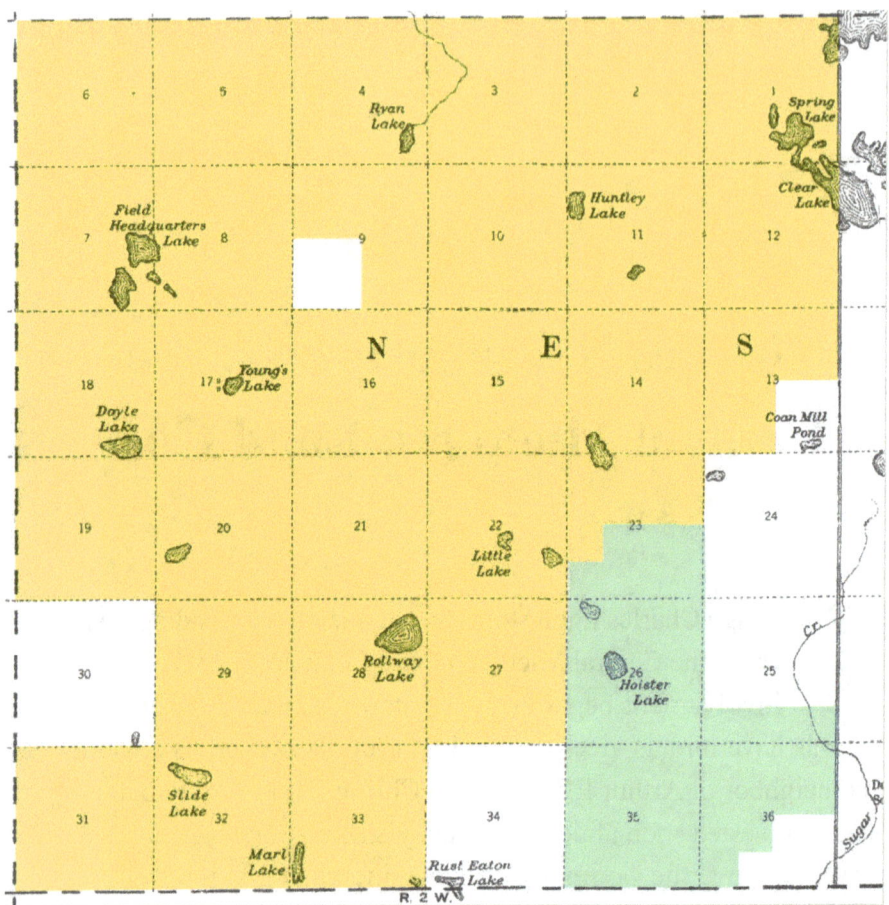

In 1912, Charles Eggleston foreclosed on a mortgage he held with the Central Michigan Land Company. The lands were auctioned off in two parcels in 1914. Charles Eggleston was the highest bidder.

when the executive committee met in Chicago on September 13, 1912. Sometime after 1912, Eggleston also paid the back taxes on the property for the years 1909–12, totaling $7,919.76.

Within months of the additional mortgage of September 1912, Eggleston began legal proceedings that would ultimately bring into his possession the greater part of West Nester Township. This was a mortgage foreclosure by sale of premises. In January of 1913,

Eggleston made notice of the company's default. Due on the mortgage was the sum of $113,341.24. Ironically, just the past June, the
Gladwin paper had declared that the firm had "unlimited capital
behind the enterprise."[2]

At one o'clock in the afternoon on Monday, April 28, 1913, a
public auction was scheduled at the front door of the Court House
in the village of Roscommon for the mortgaged property. At the
auction, the highest bid was $13,638.90. A sheriff's deed for the
property was recorded to Charles Eggleston on May 29, 1913.

On the same day that the sheriff's deed was recorded, Eggleston
filed a civil suit against the company and others. Apparently, it
would take more than just this auction and the sheriff's deed to
gain legal possession of the company's property. On February 28,
1914, the court acknowledged that the company owed Eggleston
$55,353.22, for several promissory notes, mortgages, and taxes. It
was further ruled that the company must pay this amount with 6%
interest on or before March 24, 1914. If the company defaulted on
this mortgage, the property would be sold at auction any time after
March 24, 1914. With no payment forthcoming, on April 1, a decree
was filed to auction the property.[3]

The court then ordered that on May 25 at 1:00 p.m. the property
would be sold. The sale was advertised in the *Roscommon Herald-
News* for seven weekly issues during April and May. Notices were
also posted in town on telephone poles at 5th & Lake, Main & Lake,
Brooks & Main, Brooks & 5th and on the front door of the Court
House.

The sale would be in two parts. The first part was described
as Sec 1, 2, 3, 4, 5, 6, 7, 8, N½ & SE¼ of 9, 10, 11, 12, N½ &
SW¼ of 13, 14, 15, 16, 17, 18, 19, 20, 21, 22, N½ & NW¼ of
SW¼ of 23, 27, 28, 29, 31, 32, 33 all in T. 21 N., R. 2 W. (West
Nester Township). Except for parts of sections 9 and 13, and all
of sections 30 and 34, this represented all of the present-day Clear
Lake Ranch within this township (part of the lake extends into East

Nester Township) and most of what is today Mid-Forest Lodge. Sections 30 and 34 were earlier released by Eggleston from the suit.

If needed, the following additional acreage would be sold: SW¼ of SW¼, E½ of SW¼, SE¼ of section 23, S½ of S½ of section 25, section 26, section 35, N½, N½ of SW¼ and SW¼ of SW¼ of section 36. This additional acreage represents today's Double Eagle Ranch, with the exception of the NW¼ of the SW¼ of section 23, and the SE¼ of the SW¼ and the NW¼ of the SE¼ of section 36.

The sale proceeded on May 25, 1914, on the steps of the Court House. The first parcel sold for $48,933.56 to the highest bidder: Charles Eggleston. This being insufficient to cover the debt, however, the second parcel was auctioned. Again, Eggleston was the highest bidder, paying $7,400. On June 17, 1914, an order confirming the sale was filed. A Circuit Court Commissioner's deed was executed and delivered to Eggleston. With that, it was over. Charles Eggleston and his wife now owned most of West Nester Township.

The Central Michigan Land Company had sold the second parcel to Colby Thomas in July of 1911, who then sold it to Charles H. Perrine and his wife in September of 1911. This parcel was encumbered with several mortgages originally held by Arthur E. Thomas. Having gained title to this property through the suit, Eggleston sold the parcel back to Perrine in December of 1914 with a $5,000 mortgage. This parcel was later sold, in April of 1925, to William L. Eaton of Chicago (now including the NW¼ of the SW¼ of section 23) who, in turn, sold it to Thomas D. Bell of Chicago in July of 1929. Ethyl J. Bell and her husband and Marcus A. Peiser and his wife, Leanore, sold this parcel to Michael J. Willing on January 26, 1953.[4]

CHAPTER 30

False and Fraudulent Representation

C harles B. Eggleston was dying. Ensconced at his home in Pasadena, California, ill and frail for the past few years, he had been advised by his physician to remain in California even though efforts were underway in 1919 to defraud him of all his real-estate holdings in Roscommon County.

Wealth had allowed Charles and Mary to retire to California. Having married in June of 1907, they traveled to England, returning the following December, perhaps as a belated honeymoon. Prior to this trip, he still referred to his occupation as a stockbroker, but by 1910 he was retired and claimed no occupation. Even his long-occupied home on Indiana Avenue in Chicago was sold by 1915.

In October of 1918, C. D. Hillman and Kay McKay met with Charles Eggleston to discuss a business deal involving his property in Roscommon County, Michigan. McKay claimed to be in the cattle business with George R. Smith, a wealthy businessman of Seattle. According to McKay, Smith wanted to retire and return to Michigan where early in life he had farmed. Smith wanted to set his son up in the cattle business. It was alleged that Smith had a large contract with the government to supply beef to Camp Kearney.

In exchange for his real estate holdings and other considerations, Eggleston would receive notes totaling $147,250, secured by mortgage on valuable real estate in Seattle. The Roscommon property was valued at $8.00 per acre in this transaction.

Eggleston, believing these were wealthy and reputable men and cognizant of his ill health, entered a verbal agreement. He would have to pay the back taxes on the property in Roscommon County, totaling $10,000, and provide a draft for $3,000.00 from which the buyers would pay the 1918 taxes. On November 15, 1918, he signed the deed.

In only a matter of days, Eggleston discovered that the $3,000 draft had been cashed contrary to the agreement. Eggleston immediately wrote the county clerk in an attempt to forestall the sale. Unfortunately, the clerk had already acted on the transaction and advised Eggleston that, regardless of his concern, the paperwork was in order and the clerk was compelled to register the transaction. This was done on November 22, 1918. Examination of the mortgages securing the notes had discovered them to be on wild land with no market value and all with unpaid taxes. George R. Smith was suspected to be fictitious. Hillman and McKay then tried to sell the property to an Emile Franklin Pierce of Chicago.

It is difficult to comprehend the poor judgment of this one-time adept and seasoned commission merchant and longtime member of the Chicago Board of Trade. Perhaps knowing his time was limited and not wanting to leave his wife encumbered with this far-off property, he was overly anxious to sell. It seems that, given his background and expertise, age and ill health were most likely factors in one way or another.

Eggleston began legal proceedings on February 10, 1919. Alleging that false and fraudulent representation were made respecting the promissory notes secured by the real estate mortgages, he sued to recover clear title to his property and to the $3,000. A countersuit was brought against him claiming that the land was a burden to Eggleston and worth less than believed at the time of purchase. To substantiate this claim the following was alleged: that the orchard had partially died and was grossly neglected at the time of the transaction, that the property was 15 miles from the nearest railroad or market, that it was so isolated it was difficult to hire help, that access roads were lacking, that buildings had become dilapidated, that taxes were not paid, and that settlers selling lands in Nester were doing so at sacrificial prices or leaving the township unable to sell at all.

It was also claimed that after the transaction, Eggleston tore down buildings, selling them for what he could, that he sold metal roofs for scrap, that he pastured 500 head of cattle for $1.00 per head, that he rushed a sawmill into operation to cut and sell timber from the property, that he harvested and sold apples and that he deprived the buyers from use of the property. Additionally, he was pilloried for allegedly turning on his friend Arthur Thomas. Eggleston denied all charges.

Unfortunately, Charles Brier Eggleston would die before he learned the outcome of what became an extended legal process. On May 18, 1919, Eggleston passed away in Pasadena. He was buried in Cincinnati. Mary, being the administrator of his estate, would have to continue the fight in court. Ultimately, the court decree ruled in her favor and on January 4, 1921, that decree was signed and filed. Now, Mary would have to decide the future of these extensive holdings in West Nester Township.[1]

CHAPTER 31

The School Teacher

Mary Elizabeth Farmer entered Wellesley College during its second year of enrollment in 1876. It was a rather progressive educational opportunity for a young woman from Chicago. Her father, an insurance agent, had been born in Massachusetts and, perhaps because Wellesley is located in Massachusetts, and he had only two daughters, a college education at Wellesley was within the means and aspirations of the family.[1][2]

Having procured her teaching degree, she found employment in nearby Brookline, Massachusetts, where she taught for the next 10 years. By 1890, having recently turned 30 years old, she was drawn back to Chicago. Here she followed her life's work until 1907. That year, the spouseless teacher, seemingly resigned to spinsterhood, would marry for the first time at the age of 47. Her husband was ten years her senior, the wealthy Chicagoan, Charles Brier Eggleston.[3]

One month prior to the wedding, Charles obtained a passport, apparently planning a post-wedding honeymoon. Charles and Mary did travel to Europe that year and returned from England during December of 1907. Following her marriage, Mary forsook her teaching and joined Charles in retirement. They shared his home on Indiana Avenue in Chicago and a residence in Pasadena, California.[4][5]

Mary eventually became acquainted with her husband's real estate holdings in Michigan. They spent the summer of 1912 on the Central Michigan Land Company's property in Roscommon County. This extended stay ended with their return to Chicago in November.[6]

The death of Charles Eggleston precipitated numerous changes at the Fruit Farm. Notably, the arrangement existing between

Mary Elizabeth Eggleston
(1859–1940)

Charles and Arthur Edwin Thomas for managing the Fruit Farm ended abruptly. Thomas had moved to Arizona and returned to practicing medicine by January of 1920. Velma Entrekin appears to have become the manager of Mary's property after Thomas left.[7]

Additionally, the Fruit Farm became Mary's seasonal home now that the suit over the fraudulent sale was settled and the property had become her responsibility.

Mary never remarried. She used the property as a summer home. One of her pastimes was horseback riding, and to pursue her interest, a "small riding stable was built out of pine dead head lumber from Big Headquarter's Lake." Mary, along with "her niece and guest kept their riding horses there." During the winter months, though, she still returned to the home in Pasadena that she had once shared with Charles.[8]

Overseeing such a large parcel of land would have been a daunting task for a widow and Mary must have had some hesitancy at taking this stewardship on long term, for by 1925 she was entertaining offers to sell the property. This may also have been influenced by a health issue that sent her to a hospital in Ann Arbor during the late fall of that year.[9]

In May of 1925, a Mr. Myers spent a week looking over the property with intentions of buying. No transaction materialized after this visit, and Mary had a more serious party looking in September. This time the *Detroit Free Press* reported the sale as a *fait accompli*, stating that a "tract of 18,000 acres of Michigan forest land, surrounding several lakes and adjoining a state forest reserve and a state game preserve, was purchased last week by Glover Watson organization, Dearborn subdividers, from Mrs. Mary Eggleston, a resident of Chicago."[10] [11] [12]

Rhapsodically describing the property, Mr. Watson exclaimed: "the forest cover teems with wild game, including deer, bear, fox, pheasant, partridge and ducks. Eighteen lakes on the property, many of which have not been fished for years are stocked with bass, walleye pike, muskellonge *[sic]*, and blue gills." Furthermore, he stated that the "game and fish have been protected in this territory for twenty years" and that the property "is completely enclosed with woven wire fence."[13]

Glover Watson further tallied some other existing enhancements, reporting that the "tract already is improved with a large club house and a dozen detached cottages, and caretaker's, game wardens' and guides' cottages, and a *[sic]* apple orchard of 240 acres." With the property's development in mind, Mr. Watson expounded that there were plans "to lay out golf courses and tennis courts, to be completed next summer."[14]

For whatever reason, this announcement of a sale was premature. At about the same time of the reported transaction, Mary was released from the hospital and planned, as usual, to spend the winter in Pasadena. It would be another ten years before sale of the property would be seriously considered.[15]

Regardless of the interest she received to sell the property, Mary was, throughout the 1920s and 1930s, actively consolidating her ownership in West Nester. One of the most important purchases was made in July of 1923. Mary was able to purchase from Lillian E. McCreary her property in sections 6 and 7 of East Nester Township, providing her with the remainder of Clear Lake. Other in-holdings purchased were the SW¼ of section 9 in 1925 and all of section 30 in 1931. It is no coincidence that these were the last two parcels purchased to consolidate her ownership. Agriculture was attempted on both of these parcels, but like so much of the cutover land in Northern Michigan, it was unsustainable.[16] [17]

Though it is doubtful if any of the ventures associated with this property, starting with the Central Michigan Land Company, made enough money to sustain ownership, Mary proved dogged and attempted an additional enterprise by allowing exploratory drilling for oil as early as 1927 and leasing for oil and gas throughout the 1930s. No mineral wealth was forthcoming. After this, there was no longer an expectation that this vast acreage would somehow provide a self-sustaining source of income, not that it ever really had.

Mary did, however, open the property up to deer hunters in the mid-1930s to generate some cash flow. She ran ads in the *Detroit Free Press* in the fall of 1935 soliciting hunters. The ad announced that a "new hunting camp for men has been opened on the nineteen thousand-acre tract known as the Eggleston Fruit Farm in Nestor *[sic]* Township, Roscommon County." The ad boasted that the "property has been closed to hunting for years and has been carefully patrolled." There are an "abundance of deer on this tract," it trumpeted. Prospective hunters could write to Mary for "price of permits to hunt and rate for lodging and meals."[18]

Access to Nester Township was also changing during Mary's ownership in the 1920s. The township had always been allied, socially and economically, more to Gladwin County than to Roscommon County. To the south was the township's connection to trade and communication, while to the north was a tangle of trails connecting the township to the county seat of Roscommon. In the spring of 1926, M-55 was being finished between M-76 and Houghton Lake. Two years later, the road south from the former Towner settlement (Maple Valley) was being graded over the steep hills south to Twin Lakes and Clear Lake. At the Eggleston ranch, this road would connect with the road from Gladwin. Residents, including Mary, now had a more direct route to Roscommon and West Branch.[19] [20]

In 1929, the Fruit Farm became Mary's permanent residence. Charles had been gone for ten years and Mary was nearly 70 years old. In 1930, she spent the winter in Pasadena, as usual, but stayed at the Maryland Hotel.[21] [22]

While in Pasadena, Mary was a member of The Shakespeare Club of Pasadena from 1918 until her death. Certainly, this was a needed social outlet, given the death of Charles in 1919. The mission of the club "was not only social, it was heavily geared towards the educational and cultural exposure of its members." The club was "deeply interested in civic improvements" and "philanthropic pursuits."[23]

Mary was Chairman of the December Committee for the Social Hour in 1921–22 and on the First Tuesdays Luncheon Committee during 1923–24. Club records show her Pasadena residences as 1132 South Orange Grove and then 503 South Los Robles Avenue.[24]

Childless and no doubt with her legacy in mind, Mary financially supported the construction of the Eggleston school, built in 1934 in East Nester Township. In 1996, the school was listed as a Michigan Historic Site and added to the National Register of Historic Places.[25]

During the last decade of her life, age and health required Mary to employ a full-time nurse. She also hired a new caretaker for the property. This caretaker was instrumental in facilitating the sale of the bulk of the property. On September 7, 1938, Mary signed the indenture to the Frankmore Corporation, a precursor organization that became Mid-Forest Lodge. Through her will, the caretaker would garner the headquarters remnant of the once vast Central Michigan Land Company holdings. This included sections 1 and 12, which encompassed Clear Lake.[26]

Mary died on Monday, June 10, 1940. She had been a patient at the Tolfree Memorial Hospital in West Branch since April of that year.[27]

CHAPTER 32

Native Son

I t is an abiding question to be asked of all settlers to new lands, "Whither you come?" For Holloway Buck the question is especially applicable. He left his farm in Fenton Township, Genesee County, to settle in northern Crawford County during the 1870s, the time when the Jackson, Lansing & Saginaw Railroad had just crossed the county, making its path to Mackinaw. Holloway Buck followed the railroad north bringing his wife and young family to a raw and virgin land.[1] [2]

In 1880, Holloway was just one of 29 heads of households in Maple Forest Township, most all of whom were farmers. Holloway eventually proved up an 80-acre homestead comprising the N½ of the NW¼ of section 32 in T. 28 N., R. 2 W. His father proved up the adjacent 80 acres to the east.[3] [4]

If Holloway did come for the fertile soil, he was disappointed, for both homesteads have reverted to state land today. Perhaps he was attempting to benefit from the value of the virgin timber, a one-time windfall at best.

The youngest of his four children, his son Amos, was just three years old in 1880. Amos grew up here during the time that the great lumber harvest occurred throughout the county. At 19, he was married and, like his father, farming in Maple Forest Township.[5]

No amount of effort, determination, or optimism could alter the simple fact that the soil would determine these farmers' fates. By 1910, Amos had given up farming and taken to the woods to earn a wage as a log scaler in Roscommon Township, probably at the new town of Michelson. He was involved as an elector when Lake

Amos Alfred Buck
(1877–1963)

Township was created in 1912, undoubtedly due to the growth of Michelson. He was supervisor of the township while living at Michelson in 1916.[6][7][8]

As early as 1919, Amos was one of the directors from Roscommon County of the Northeastern Michigan Development

Bureau. This organization claimed in 1919 that its sole objective was "to advertise the resources, advantages and possibilities of Northeastern Michigan — agricultural, horticultural and industrial, earnestly and without exaggeration." Amos was part of the effort in these counties to find uses for cutover lands, especially agricultural.[9] [10]

Amos must have been an industrious worker for, by 1920, he was the manager of the Michelson Lumber Company. Its sawmill at Michelson was in operation from 1909 to 1924. Amos stayed in Michelson after the closing of the mill and in 1930 was a proprietor of a lumberyard, Amos Buck Lumber Company.[11] [12] [13]

Amos was a prominent enough citizen of Roscommon County to be asked to welcome the Michigan Press Association to Johnston's Rustic Tavern Dining Hall in 1927. As an advocate for the county, Amos told the crowd of 250 to 300 guests: "there is no people who appreciate the privilege of entertaining the Michigan Press association and their ladies as do the people of Houghton Lake. This section has the best fishing in the United States, good motoring over good roads, golfing, dancing, etc. If you can find entertainment and contentment in these, we give them to you."[14]

For some years in the 1930s, Amos was an elected official with the Roscommon County Road Commission. He served as chairman in 1931. He represented Roscommon County on the Northern Michigan Road Commissioners Association in 1930 serving as the Vice-President.[15] [16]

Sometime during the 1930s, Amos was employed by Mary Eggleston to help manage her vast holdings in Nester Township. As caretaker, he oversaw the property and building maintenance, kept trespassers out and supervised oil and gas leases. Most importantly, Amos assisted with the sale of the bulk of the property and the eventual creation of Mid-Forest Lodge.[17]

After her death in 1940, Mary Eggleston left the remainder of her property around Clear Lake to Amos. He continued to live on the

Clear Lake property and remained involved in Mid-Forest Lodge for many years. He served as president as early as 1940.[18]

Amos's first wife, Lillian, filed for divorce in April of 1941, claiming abandonment. It was granted on July 1, 1941. Soon after,

Amos (on right) and Louise Buck sold the remaining West Nester property around Clear Lake to three Detroit businessmen (Leo Lapwing pictured here) in September 1953. The last tie to the Egglestons and the Central Michigan Land Company is severed.

on July 25, 1941, Amos married the housekeeper/nurse Louise Wellman, who had been working for Mary Eggleston up until her death.[19] [20]

Amos and Louise continued to live on the property but sold off some of the land on the east side of F-97 and parts of section 1. In September of 1953, they sold the remaining property encompassing

Clear Lake and the original headquarters and orchard of the Central Michigan Land Company to three Detroit businessmen.

Amos had spent his whole life in the north woods; grown up during the great lumber era, struggled as a farmer on substandard soil, witnessed the rise and fall of Michelson over its twenty-year existence, owned and operated a lumber company store, helped establish and oversee an enduring hunting and fishing club and, at the age of 76, retired to an apartment in Grand Rapids. He lived another ten years, Louise another twenty-one.

CHAPTER 33

Passing the Baton

F or any given parcel of land in West Nester Township, there is a trail of ownership leading up to the present day. Throughout this book some of these transfers have been discussed but no one parcel has been followed in its entirety.

Prior to the Treaty of Saginaw in 1819, West Nester Township was part of a large section of lower Michigan owned by Native Americans. This treaty with the Chippewa, Ottawa, and Potawatomi tribes brought more than six million acres into federal ownership.

Not until the 1860s did lands within West Nester Township move from the federal government into private hands as seen in chapter two. To illuminate the succession of ownership, section 12 will be utilized as an example. Though this tale could be told for any section of West Nester Township, section 12 was one of only 13 sections known to have never been subdivided, keeping the trail of ownership simple and concise.

As seen in chapter two, Jefferson F. Bundy and John G. Lowman were the original patentees of section 12. Their purchase on September 5, 1866, began this section's history of private ownership. The heirs of Jefferson F. Bundy (he died in 1874) and John G. Lowman (as well as the estate of his brother Hovey) held ownership until October 11, 1876. On that date, by action of the circuit court of the county of Roscommon, section 12 passed into new hands.

The court had ruled on May 24, 1876, owing to a delinquent mortgage dated March 5, 1872, that the mortgaged premises, including section 12, would be sold at public auction to cover the principal, interest, and costs of the foreclosure suit.

Mortgage holders included Peter Mumford, Martin Watrous, J. Arthur Bailey, Benjamin F. Orton and David G. Slafter. Though David G. Slafter was a mortgage holder, he was also the highest bidder at the public auction in Houghton Lake. He paid $6,939.33 for the 1,528 acres involved, including section 12.

The mortgage holders all had ties to the Saginaw Valley. During the 1870s, Peter Mumford (1827–1895) was involved in the lumber business in Saginaw, owning a planing mill in that county. Martin Watrous (1804–1877) also had ties to the lumber industry; his mill was in Bay City during the 1870s. J. Arthur Bailey and Benjamin F. Orton were partners in a hardware concern in Saginaw and Bay City during the 1870s. David G. Slafter (1817–1908) was a prominent citizen of Tuscola County. He was a justice of the peace, banker, lumberman and involved in real estate.

Two days after his purchase on October 13, 1876, Slafter sold a one-third interest in the 1,528 acres for $2,313.11 to Mary M. Mumford (1822–1893), Peter's wife. Thomas Nester would buy Mary M. Mumford's one-third interest in these parcels and others (3,128 acres) in West Nester Township six days after her purchase, on October 19, 1876, for $10,426.67.

Finally, on October 21, 1876, Thomas Nester bought the remaining interest in both groups of parcels (3,128 acres) from David G. Slafter, J. Arthur Bailey, Benjamin F. Orton, and John J. Wheeler for $24,510. Slafter's other partners only held an interest in the second group of parcels.

As detailed in chapter seven, "The Big Sale," Thomas Nester held section 12 until he sold out to Wright, Wells and Stone on December 27, 1881. As mentioned in chapter eight, in 1883, Wright pooled all his interests into the Wright Lumber Company, bringing section 12 under its umbrella.

The company did not pay taxes on section 12 in 1897, 1898 or 1899, the timber having been harvested. Most likely, the section reverted to the state in 1899/1900 for nonpayment of taxes. Tax titles for these lands in Roscommon County would be held by the Auditor General of Michigan.

Roscommon County was one of many northern counties burdened with a surfeit of cutover land. Dealing with this abundance would ultimately give rise to the state forest reserves, a predecessor of Michigan's state forests.

Though Roscommon County was one of the counties that gave birth to the new reserves, John Carter from Chicago would purchase tax titles from the Auditor General for tens of thousands of acres in Roscommon County in 1902, before they were swept up into the reserves. He paid the Roscommon County treasurer for a certificate to purchase the rights of the State in these lands held by the Auditor General. On May 6, 1902, he did this for section 12. So began the long process of obtaining clear title for this tax-reverted section. As it turns out, Carter had only purchased these titles based on the back taxes of 1897 and 1898.

Carter sold his tax-title interest in most of West Nester Township, including section 12, to Nathaniel Robinson and Louis Auer about a year later, on May 16, 1903.

On August 18, 1903, Robinson and Auer bought 5,920 acres in West Nester Township from the Wright Lumber Company for one dollar, including section 12. This was their effort to buy up all the original titles and make theirs perfect.

As seen in chapters 16 and 17, during September of 1904, Robinson and Auer sold a one-half interest in their West Nester parcels to Arthur E. Thomas and his brother Wesley M. Thomas. The four partners would, that same month, transfer the lands to their newly formed concern, the Central Michigan Land Company.

Clean title still escaped the partners, however. The lands had not been redeemed as the law provided. Apparently, the taxes for 1899 needed to be paid before the Auditor General could clear title. On April 18, 1905, John Carter obtained a new title from the Auditor General. Having paid the county treasurer additional funds, he presented a new certificate to the Auditor General and, in the same indenture, assigned the title to Robinson and Auer. Title to section 12 was now perfect.

As we have seen in previous chapters, Charles Eggleston and his wife would, by foreclosure, receive the title to section 12 in 1914. At the death of Charles in 1919, Mary (having settled the lawsuit) became sole owner until her death in 1940. Amos Buck received section 12 as bequeathed in Mary's will.

Two of the three businessmen who purchased section 12 from Amos Buck in 1953, Leo. J. Lapwing and Elator Kotwick, held section 12 until June 10, 1996.

The tale of section 12 is no outlier compared to most of the lands in West Nester Township. From its first purchase in 1866, it was held by land investors speculating on future appreciation based on the standing timber until the timber was harvested in 1893–6.

It is questionable if any of these owners ever set foot on section 12 — even Thomas Nester may have never visited it. He sold it before lumber operations were even being considered in that corner of his ownership. All these owners relied on land lookers to assess their investment. It is possible that, until it was purchased as tax delinquent land, no owner visited this section.[1]

CHAPTER 34

Green Gold

The great wealth of the virgin forests was a one-time gift of nature. For the lumbermen who arrived in Saginaw, Grand Haven, or Muskegon during the 1850s and 1860s, some were able to position themselves to harvest this wealth in the upper reaches of the Saginaw and Muskegon drainages, where railroads would be required. By the 1870s and 1880s these early arrivers had the experience, capital, and connections to accomplish this.

As has often been noted, in "dollar value, Michigan's 'green gold' out-valued California's 'yellow gold' by more than a billion dollars." So, who really profited from the "green gold" in West Nester Township? And what happened to these fortunes?[1]

Of course, many of these gentlemen have been introduced already, but their life after the West Nester harvest has not been discussed.

Regarding the Nester/Wright operation, there are seven individuals who held ownership at one time or another: Thomas Nester, Charles William Wells, Farnum Chickering Stone, Oscar Daniel Wetherell, William Hale Wright, Willis Taylor Knowlton, and Ammi Willard Wright.

First and foremost, is Thomas Nester. After the great sale, Thomas Nester turned his focus to Michigan's Upper Peninsula. In eight years, he developed his mill in Baraga and began harvesting timber in the region. In that time, he constructed a network of logging railroads and built and purchased a fleet of lake vessels. He was described as "ruddy-faced and powerfully built, with black hair and grey eyes twinkling with good humor and personally he was a most companionable gentleman."[2]

On Saturday, May 10, 1890, Nester was overcome by a fit of apoplexy while walking on his trams that extended out over L'Anse Bay at his mill in Baraga. He died two days later.

Unlike the two-dimensional archetypic lumbermen, he was no blindly avaricious businessman. "He was a real Auld Sod Irishman that was fond of a joke." Truly, "everybody who had business dealings with Nester would swear by him." Described as "genial, broadminded, whole-souled, Thomas Nester was a man among men and he made his life count for good and for genuine helpfulness." At his death, the Marquette paper stated that he "was an excellent example of the progress to fortune that may be made in this country by a man possessing only native energy and determination at the start."[3][4][5]

After the death of Thomas Nester, the business continued as "the Estate of Thomas Nester." At his death, and with all debt accounted for, the estate was valued at approximately 1.5 million dollars. His sons, particularly George, his oldest, would continue management of the estate and business. The estate lasted for over twenty more years, harvesting the original tracts Thomas Nester had purchased, and going on to operate in Minnesota and even Ontario.[6]

Thomas's widow, Margaret, lived with her son George until her death in 1922. Four children survived childhood. George died of a stroke, as had his father, just days before his mother on April 15, 1922. Mary Ann (Bourke) survived until 1941. John died while engaged with the business of the estate in 1913. Francis Patrick (Frank) outlived them all, passing in 1951.

The family's wealth dissipated by the third generation.

• • • • •

Charles William Wells came to Saginaw in 1867 and became involved with the lumbermen's supply business. He was ultimately one of the prominent associates cultivated by Ammi Wright. He was most identified with Wells, Stone & Co., though his business involvements were numerous. These included the lumbering operations in West Nester Township before and after Thomas Nester was bought out. With Wright, he pursued the lumber trade into Minnesota.[7]

It was in Itasca County, Minnesota, that Wells, along with three friends and six guides, travelled to remote Bowstring Lake for a month-long hunting expedition. There, on October 18, 1893, he died after falling into the water from his canoe as he shot at some passing ducks. Clinging to the boat while the guide (Dan MacIntosh) propelled it toward shore, he suffered an apparent heart attack and exclaimed "My God, MacIntosh, I'm perishing." He was 52 years old.[8]

As his wife had died the year before, the bulk of his estate was directed to his two daughters, Jean and Helen. The will requested that his business interest "continue for a period of fifteen years, unless in the judgement of the executors they should be sooner terminated." The estate was claimed to be worth $3,000,000.[9][10]

The two daughters married and stayed in Saginaw. Both lived well judging from census and travel records. Jean passed in 1947, Helen in 1930.

• • • • •

Like Charles Wells, Farnum Chickering Stone came to Saginaw in 1867 and began a lifelong career in the lumber supply business. He entered the employ of Northup, Wells & Company and soon became a partner of the reorganized and renamed company: Wells, Stone

& Company. His business involvement blossomed well beyond this initial firm. He held ownership in "Stone, Nester & Company, Thomas Nester & Company, A. W. Wright & Company, with Willis T. Knowlton and others, the Swan River Logging Company, Wright, Davis & Company, with Charles H. Davis and Gilbert M. Stark."[11]

Farnum Stone died of pneumonia on December 5, 1893. He "was taken ill shortly after the death of his beloved associate in business, Maj. C. W. Wells." His estate was "valued at upwards of $1,000,000."[12][13]

The Stone estate was managed by partner, Ammi Wright, his wife, Harriet F. Stone, and his oldest son, Edwin P. Stone. Edwin became the "manager of the affairs of Wells, Stone & Co., under A.W. Wright." He remained in the lumber business into the 1930s.[14]

Harriet stayed in Saginaw and passed in 1908. The children all lived into the 1940s. Edwin died in 1943, George and Kittie Louise in 1941.

· · · · ·

Unlike the other partners, Oscar Daniel Wetherell was not from Michigan. He was a prominent lumberman from Chicago. Born in 1834, he arrived in that city at the age of nineteen. By the 1870s he was in the lumber business and owned a lumberyard and planing mill in that city. In Saginaw, he was an early partner with Ammi and William Wright in a lumber mill. He eventually became involved in banking and was a long-serving city official. A portrait of Chicago's public officials in 1896 stated that his "successes in life have not been confined to the domain of lumber. Few men have of late years been more potent and influential in shaping the affairs of this great city." In 1898, he removed to Tampa, Florida, and had a second career as a real-estate developer. He died in 1911.[15]

From his two marriages, six children and his second wife survived him.

From his first marriage, his daughter Mary died a widow in 1931, while daughter Ester, divorced and living with her own daughter, died in 1935.

His second wife, Harriet, outlived Oscar by more than twenty years, dying in Florida in 1932, where her home had been valued at $50,000 two years earlier.

From the second marriage, four children survived beyond 1911. The oldest, Robert, retired from his career as a country club manager in 1957 and died the following year. His daughter, Sybil, married a banker and lived until 1978. According to census records, Oscar Daniel Jr. was manager of a wholesale liquor business in 1940. He died in 1958. The youngest child to outlive Oscar was Louise, whose husband was a bookkeeper; he passed in 1965 and she in 1981.

• • • • •

William Hale Wright was the younger brother of Ammi Wright. In 1845, at the age of 18, he left Vermont and came to Michigan. He trained as a carpenter for twelve years before coming to the Saginaw Valley. There he began a new career in the lumber business. He was first employed by his brother in Bay City and eventually became a member of his brother's company. Ultimately, when his brother's company was incorporated, he "was the fourth largest stockholder in the company."[16]

William died in 1893, but during "the more than thirty years of active business life in Saginaw, Mr. Wright was esteemed by his associates as an honest, upright, sagacious business man."[17]

One child from his first marriage, Mary Catherine, survived him and at the time of his death was living in New York. It seems she lived a long life and never married.

His second wife and four of their children outlived William. The wife, Jane, stayed in Saginaw, dying in 1922.

Their eldest two children, Harriet and Robert, lived with their mother until her death and remained single throughout their lives. Robert died in 1939, Harriet in 1942.

The next child, Jesse, married an accomplished civil engineer, eventually settling in Ann Arbor. She passed in 1960, outliving her husband by almost 30 years.

The youngest child, Ellen, married an insurance agent who died in 1911. She was still living in Saginaw in 1915.

· · · · ·

Willis T. Knowlton, another acolyte of Ammi Wright, after working for Wright since 1874, was invited into a partnership with Wright in his lumberyard and planing mill. When all the businesses of Ammi Wright were consolidated into the Ammi Wright Lumber Company in 1882, Knowlton subsequently benefited from the continuing West Nester harvest.

After the lumbering was finished in Michigan and Minnesota, Mr. Knowlton still "gave personal attention to Mr. Wright's individual interests and was named by him as one of the executors and trustees of his will."[18]

Willis Knowlton died in 1925 in Pasadena, California, having outlived all of his partners in the Ammi Wright Lumber Company. His wife, Grace, lived until 1933. The census in 1930 shows her in Pasadena living with three servants in a home worth $40,000.

His two daughters, Carrie and Helen, lived into their eighties, passing in 1969 and 1974, respectively. Both lived, according to census records, in homes with servants in 1930 and 1940.

· · · · ·

There are probably few, if any, men whose careers span as deeply and broadly the white pine era of the Saginaw basin as

Ammi Willard Wright. He settled in Saginaw in 1851 and rode the tide of the great lumber boom by his diligence and business acumen. He was involved in every aspect of the lumber trade, harvesting the pine, manufacturing lumber, selling wholesale lumbermen's supplies and selling and distributing finished lumber. His partners and the companies he formed were numerous and prominent.

Unlike Nester, Wells and Stone, Wright outlived the Saginaw lumber boom and enjoyed his wealth late into his life. He was 89 when he died in 1912, leaving his wife and family well taken care of financially.

His estate was conservatively valued at slightly more than $5,000,000. The bulk of his estate, after a ten-year period, went to his only surviving child, Sarah. Wright biographer David McMacken stated that considering "how much Sarah inherited, it is amazing to realize that at her death she left very little money. The millions that Ammi Wright had amassed as a shrewd and prudent businessman— Sarah and Henry (her husband) had spent." Fortunately, Wright left $10,000 to each of his four grandchildren when they attained 21 years of age. Sarah died in 1947, her husband in 1934.[19]

• • • • •

Principals in the Roscommon Lumber Company included Healy Cady Akeley, Charles Boyden, Samuel B. Barker, George Sinclair, Thomas Morris, and Charles B. Field.

The driving force behind the company was H. C. Akeley. He was a prominent lumberman from Grand Haven, Michigan, when he formed the Roscommon Lumber Company. When the company was finished, Akeley had already set his sights on Minnesota. He was as successful in Minnesota as he had been in Michigan.

Akeley's first wife, Henrietta, died in 1907. They had one daughter from this union who would survive them. Akeley remarried in

October of 1911 at the age of 75. His new wife, Clara Rood Royce, was 40.

Like Ammi Wright, Akeley would live long enough to retire and enjoy life. Also, like Wright he died in 1912. He left behind his daughter and new wife of nine months.

Clara remained a widow. She died on January 1, 1947, leaving a substantial portion of her estate to charity. Akeley's daughter, Florence Henrietta Akeley, born in 1878, married in 1904. She had one son and was divorced by 1920. By 1940, she was renting a home in California and sharing it with one lodger. She passed in 1956.

•••••

Charles E. Boyden came to Grand Haven, Michigan, in 1871 and eventually became connected with H. C. Akeley. In 1882, they owned and operated the "largest shingle mill in the world, with a capacity of 1,000,000 shingles and 50,000 feet of lumber daily."[20]

In 1890, Boyden purchased timberland in southern Missouri and erected a large mill in Neeleyville. It was at this mill that he died inspecting some new machinery. He was only 53 years old. He left an estate estimated to be worth $1,000,000.

His widow, Jerusha, returned to Grand Haven to live, passing in 1913. His oldest daughter married a lumberman and by 1920 had settled in southern California where she passed in 1955. His son John was active in the Missouri operation and lived there until the 1930s. By 1940, he was living in Chicago. He died in 1957. The youngest child, Charles, spent most of his life in California, dying in 1960.

•••••

Samuel Burns Barker was involved in the lumber business most of his life. By 1880, he was a notable lumber dealer in Chicago. He was a logical choice for H. C. Akeley to have as a partner in the Roscommon Lumber Company for Barker could market the finished goods coming out of Michigan from their harvest in Roscommon County.

Barker stayed in the lumber business in Chicago but in 1893 his business, like many concerns, suffered from the panic that year. Barker's company failed with a debt of over $50,000 "due to stringency of the money market and the inability to secure extension of loans."[21]

In 1900, Barker was living in Manhattan where he died in 1903. He outlived his one child, a daughter, who only lived into her twenties. His widow, Aura, passed in 1914, having lived the last nine years of her life with a relative.[22]

• • • • •

Another Chicagoan who was a large stockholder of the Roscommon Lumber Company was George Franklin Sinclair. At the age of 22, in 1870, he was a lumber broker in Chicago. It was a trade he would follow until 1887. By 1882 he had become partners with H. C. Akeley and Thomas G. Morris in the firm Sinclair, Morris & Co. "For several years this firm carried on one of the largest wholesale and commission lumber operations which has ever been carried on by any one firm in this country."[23]

In 1887, Sinclair left the lumber trade and relocated to Grand Rapids, Michigan. Here he organized two companies, one for house-furnishing and another which made "an exclusive business of the manufacturing of metal furniture trimmings."[24]

Married in 1875, Sinclair had no children and outlived his wife. When he died in 1915 at the age of 68, it had been 28 years since the Roscommon Lumber Company dissolved.

• • • • •

Thomas Gurley Morris was another Chicagoan with deep ties to the lumber trade. He began work in a Chicago lumberyard when he was sixteen. Eight years later he was a bookkeeper. Ambitious and driven, a year later he opened a lumberyard in Kansas. He returned to Chicago in three years. In 1879, he shifted roles within the lumber business, becoming a commissioned merchant in that trade.[25]

He joined the partners in the Roscommon Lumber Company while maintaining his involvement in the lumber trade. He died in 1908, a lumberman to the end. He was 62. His wife, Julia, lived off of her own income until passing in 1937.

There were three children. The oldest, Ida, was born in 1872 and lived until the 1940s. His one son, Thomas Gardner, was born in 1874 and spent most of his career in Chicago. He retired to San Francisco in 1932 and lived until 1945. Their youngest daughter, Faith, born in 1886, passed away in 1938. None of the children evinced a lavish lifestyle.

• • • • •

Of all the partners in the Roscommon Lumber Company, none was more involved in the woods then Charles Byron Field.

Charles was a farmer in Vermontville, Michigan, who by 1880 had moved to Muskegon. Here he was superintendent of the boom company. Given his background and the fact that he was the only partner to work in the woods, he may have been only a minor stockholder.

After the Roscommon Lumber Company was dissolved, Charles remained in the industry, but located to Arkansas. By at least 1893, however, he had returned to Michigan and was living in Grand Rapids. Here he was president of the Michigan Sand Brick Company until 1897. He died in 1906, having been retired for several years.

Married in 1859, his wife, Helen Maria, only outlived Charles by two years. Two children survived the parents, a son Charles Henry and a daughter Stella J.

Charles Henry lived in Grand Rapids and by 1920 was president of a manufacturing company dealing in brass. He died in 1925 at the age of 58. Stella stayed in Muskegon, married, and died at age 54. Neither appeared to lead an extravagant lifestyle.

• • • • •

Though no family wealth has survived to this day, some legacy continues in the public domain. Ammi Wright's generosity lives on in Alma College. Likewise, the Akeley Memorial Building in Stowe, Vermont, reflects the philanthropic interests of Healy Cady Akeley. However, these two individuals' largesse cannot be directly attributable to their operations in West Nester Township. Their sources of income were broad and spanned decades.

The one-time wealth generated from the harvest of the virgin forest in West Nester Township did not endure in any noteworthy fashion. The West Nester lumbermen and families confirm the old adage: "shirtsleeves to shirtsleeves in three generations."

AUTHOR'S NOTE

The February winds bite at my cheeks with the added discomfort from the bead-like snow pellets cutting nearly horizontally. These hills seldom have visitors especially in such inhospitable conditions.

Yet, there are stalwart witnesses even now. Jutting out above the snow is the ubiquitous evidence of a magnificent forest. The snow beads fly across the crust, diverted by these gray-black stumps.

Forests such as these were described by Tim Nester reminiscing in 1902, "what trees they were! Why, we passed them by if they ran more than four to the thousand. Yes, sir, that pine that grew on the eastern slope of Michigan was absolutely the best that ever grew."[1]

Now there is only the silent soliloquy of their presence. They still have stories to tell but their susurrations are not quite audible. That these witnesses even survive is due to their resinous nature and char-like preservation from fires in the years following the harvest. Their size (diameter) and density provide a not inscrutable view of that long-ago forest. They were magnificent. Exceptional specimens could reach over 350 years old, 180+ feet tall and 6.5 feet in diameter.

Though the earliest murmurings of environmental concerns were already in the air at that time, industry inertia was unstoppable. They were slated for harvest and the shanty boys came with toothy bands of steel in hand, their undercuts and back cuts still clearly distinct.

Seemingly, these stumps will last forever. Yet someday they will be silenced by time, and future visitors will be unable to hear their stories.

ACKNOWLEDGMENTS

W hat spawns a book like this? It was a historical vacuum that provided the impetus for such a local, small, and focused topic. Couple that with a lifetime measure of curiosity and there it is. But any project owes a great debt to others beyond the author.

My journey as a historian would not have begun if not for the kindness, generosity, and mentorship of my friend, David McMacken, who was one of the rare individuals to also harbor an interest in this area. We published several articles relevant to West Nester. Unfortunately, he passed before he could participate in this project.

Another friend, Steve Griffin, reviewed the manuscript. His editorial advice helped shape the project. He removed most of the rough edges. My niece, Julie VanWagenen, formatted the whole project. She brought it to life as an actual book. She also created the custom maps and illustrations. Both my sister, Lanette VanWagenen, and Julie VanWagenen also reviewed the manuscript for errors in grammar and spelling.

The staff at the Clark Historical Library assisted with researching the Boyce Lumber Company Records.

Several others assisted in small ways that they have probably forgotten, given the interminable timeframe. This list includes Evelyn Down, Cory Highfield, Carl Bajema, Sue Kroes, Betsy Coleman, Ken Kilkka, Rebecca Dexter, and George Corlew. Gratitude is due all.

Lastly, I want to thank my family, especially Kathy, for tolerating all the absences to visit libraries, archives, county offices, etc.

APPENDIX 1

Throughout this text the names of certain locations, rail-roads, lakes, etc. changed over time and varied based on user (such as a given newspaper). For clarification, those with multiple references are listed below. Some of these names may not have been utilized in this text but can be found in use elsewhere.

1) Lake Thomas & Tittabawassee Railroad
   Thomas Nester Railroad
   Wells, Stone & Co. Railroad
   Wright Lumber Company Railroad*

2) Houghton Lake & Barker City Railroad
   Roscommon Lumber Company Railroad
   Charles B. (C. B.) Field's Railroad
   Field's Railroad

3) Lake Thomas
   Achill Lake
   Hoister Lake
   Atchel Lake (Used on current maps)

---

* This does not include the Wright Lumber Company Lines for the Clear Lake Harvest

4) Thomas Nester's Headquarters on Lake Thomas
   Brundage
   Nestor
   Achill (Postal Name)
   Achill

5) Conner's Lake
   Nester Lake
   Pine Lake
   Rollway Lake (Used on current maps)

6) Field's Headquarters Lake
   Field Headquarters Lake
   Headquarters Lake (Used on current maps)

7) Spider Lake
   Doyle Lake (Used on current maps)

8) Roscommon Lumber Company's Headquarters
   on Headquarters Lake
   Barker City
   Charles Field's Headquarters
   Field's Headquarters
   Nolan (Postal Name)[†]
   Old Nolan
   Mid-Forest Lodge Club House/Office
   The above are all close, if not the exact same locations.

[†]   The Nolan post office existed at this location from May of 1891 to September
       of 1899 when it was relocated to East Nester Township.

9) Wright Lumber Company Camp (On Clear Lake)
    Central Michigan Land Company Headquarters
    Jacwac (Postal Name)
    Verncroft (Postal Name)
    Eggleston Home
    Clear Lake Ranch Big House
    The above are all close, if not the exact same locations.

10) Wright Lake
    Clear Lake (Used on current maps)

11) Prudenville (Current use)
    Edna

12) Central Michigan Land Company's Holdings
    Milwaukee Fruit Farm
    Milwaukee Peach Farm
    Roscommon County Fruit Farm
    Thomas Ranch
    Fruit Farm
    Eggleston Farm

APPENDIX 2

P ost Offices located in Nester Township

Post Office	Location	Postmaster	Period of service to Nester Township
Achill	West Nester Township Section 26	Charles W. Meyers: Dec. 10, 1878–Jan. 10, 1882 James H. McDonald: Jan. 11, 1882–Sep. 19, 1882 Charles W. Meyers: Sep. 20, 1882–Jun. 11, 1884	Dec. 10, 1878–Jun. 11, 1884 Discontinued, mail to Meredith
Nolan	West Nester Township Section 7	William Finley: Jun. 11, 1891–Sep. 28, 1893 Alexander Robinson: Sep. 29, 1893–Sep. 7, 1899	Jun. 12, 1891–Sep. 7, 1899
	East Nester Township Section 19	Edward A. Coan: Sep. 8, 1899–Jul. 30, 1910	Sep. 8, 1899–Jul. 30, 1910 Discontinued, mail to Butman

Jacwac	West Nester Township Section 12	Albert A. Thomas: Dec. 18, 1909–May 31, 1910	Dec. 18, 1909–May 31, 1910 Discontinued, mail to Butman
Verncroft	West Nester Township Section 12	Carrie C. Thomas: Sep. 26, 1914–Apr. 15, 1921	Sep. 26, 1914–Apr. 15, 1921 Discontinued, mail to Gladwin

National Archives, Records Group 28: Records of the Post Office Department, 1773-1971. Series: Records of Appointment of Postmasters and the Establishment of Post Offices, File Unit: Postmaster Appointments for Roscommon County Michigan.

NOTES

Introduction

1   John C. Porter, *Mid-Forest Lodge* (Private Publication, 1969).
2   Wilbert B. Hinsdale, *Archaeological Atlas of Michigan* (Ann Arbor: University of Michigan Press, 1931).

CHAPTER 1. "The Water Pure and Deep"

1   *Survey notes.* Roscommon County Clerk's office, Roscommon, Michigan.
2   *The Sunday Sentinel* (Milwaukee, WI): January 29, 1899, Section II, 1.
3   *Survey notes.* Roscommon County Clerk's office, Roscommon, Michigan.
4   Ibid.
5   Ibid.
6   John S. Burt, *They Left Their Mark. A Biography of William Austin Burt* (Rancho Cordova, California: Landmark Enterprises, 1985).

CHAPTER 2. A Land-Office Business

1   *Jackson, Lansing & Saginaw Railroad Co. Guide to the Lands of the Jackson, Lansing & Saginaw Railroad Co. in Michigan* (Lansing, Michigan: W.S. George & Co., 1883).
2   Silas Farmer, *History of Detroit and Wayne County and Early Michigan* (New York: Munsell & Co., 1890).
3   Truman B. Fox, *History of the Saginaw Valley, its Resources, Progress and Business Interests* (East Saginaw, Michigan: Daily Courier Steam Job Print, 1868).
4   *A Biographical Record of Chemung County New York* (New York and Chicago: The S. J. Clarke Publishing Company, 1902).
5   James Cooke Mills, *History of Saginaw County Michigan, Volume II* (Saginaw, Michigan: Seeman & Peters, Publishers, 1918).
6   Silas Farmer, *History of Detroit and Wayne County and Early Michigan* (New York: Munsell & Co., 1890).

7   *The City of Detroit Michigan, 1701–1922, Volume IV* (Detroit-Chicago: The S.J. Clarke Publishing Company, 1922).

8   *Proceedings of the Thirtieth Annual Meeting of the Fire Underwriter's Association of the Northwest. Chicago, IL., September 27-28, 1899* (Milwaukee, Wis.: King-Cramer Co., Printers and Engravers, 1899).

9   *Jackson, Lansing & Saginaw Railroad Co. Guide to the Lands of the Jackson, Lansing & Saginaw Railroad Co. in Michigan* (Lansing, Michigan: W.S. George & Co., 1883).

10 Cuyler Reynolds, ed., *Hudson-Mohawk Genealogical and Family Memoirs, Volume II* (New York: Lewis Historical Publishing Company, 1911).

11 *Biographical History of Genesee County Michigan* (Indianapolis: B. F. Bowen & Co., Publishers, 1908).

12 *Men and Women of America, A Biographical Dictionary of Contemporaries* (New York City: L.R. Hammersly & Company, 1910).

13 Charles Moore, *History of Michigan, Volume III & IV* (Chicago: The Lewis Publishing Company, 1915).

14 James Cooke Mills, *History of Saginaw County Michigan, Volume II* (Saginaw, Michigan: Seeman & Peters, Publishers, 1918).

15 Western Biographical Publishing Company, *American Biographical History of Eminent and Self-Made Men* (Cincinnati: J.S. Morgan & Co., 1878).

16 *History of Saginaw County Michigan* (Chicago: Chas. C. Chapman & Co., 1881).

17 *Michigan Pioneer and Historical Society. Historical Collections, Vol. XXVI* (Lansing, MI: Robert Smith & Co., 1896).

18 *Gladwin County Record*, September 25, 1896, 5.

19 Ronald D. Swoope, *Twentieth Century History of Clearfield County Pennsylvania and Representative Citizens* (Chicago, Ill: Richmond-Arnold Publishing Co., 1911).

20 James Cooke Mills, *History of Saginaw County Michigan, Volume II* (Saginaw, Michigan: Seeman & Peters, Publishers, 1918).

21 Ibid.

22 *History of Genesee County Michigan* (Philadelphia: Everts & Abbott, 1879).

23 Archives of Michigan, Maurice Quinn Collection, Control Number 77-116.

24 Tract Books, State of Michigan, Roscommon County. Microfilm Collection. Library of Michigan.

CHAPTER 3. The Road to Houghton Lake

1   Acts of the Legislature of the State of Michigan, passed at the Regular Session of 1863, Act No. 176. (Lansing: John A Kerr & Co., Printers to the State, 1863).

2   Acts of the Legislature of the State of Michigan, passed at the Regular Session of 1867, Act No. 420. (Lansing: John A Kerr & Co., Printers to the State, 1867).

3   *Saginaw Enterprise*, August 27, 1868, 3.

4   Ibid.

5   Ibid.

6   Ibid.

7   Ibid., April 1, 1869, 1.

8   Ibid., June 17, 1869, 4.

9   Ibid., September 9, 1869, 4.

10   Ibid., September 16, 1869, 4.

11   Ibid., November 18, 1869, 5.

12   Ibid., June 17, 1869, 4.

13   *Gladwin County Record*, October 31, 1884, 1.

14   Ibid.

CHAPTER 4. "The Greatest Project in Northern Michigan"

1   *The Saginaw Courier-Herald*, May 13, 1890, 2.

2   Ibid.

3   *The Detroit Tribune*, May 13, 1890, 6.

4   *The First Logging Railroads in the Great Lakes Region. Forest & Conservation History* 35, no. 2 (April 1991): 76-83.

5   *Gladwin County Record*, April 2, 1878, 2.

6   Ibid.

7   Ibid., June 18, 1878, 3.

8   Ibid., April 2, 1878, 2.

9   Ibid., April 16, 1878, 3.

10   Land Transfer Records, Roscommon County Clerk's Office, Roscommon, Michigan.

11   *Gladwin County Record*, April 16, 1878, 3.

12   Ibid., April 16, 1878, 3.

13   Ibid.

14   Ibid., April 9, 1878, 3.

15   Ibid., June 18, 1878, 3.

16   Ibid., August 1, 1879, 3.

17   Ibid., April 2, 1880, 3.

18   Ibid., June 18, 1878, 3.

19   Ibid.

20   Ibid.

21   Ibid., May 21, 1878, 3.

22 Ibid., June 25, 1878, 3.

23 Ibid., June 18, 1878, 3.

24 Ibid., June 11, 1878, 2.

25 *Record of the Appointments of Postmasters, 1832–Sept. 30 1971, Mich.,* Volume 54, ca. 1878-96 (National Archives, Copy, State Library of Michigan).

26 *Gladwin County Record*, August 20, 1878, 3.

27 Ibid., September 24, 1878, 5.

28 Ibid., November 5, 1878, 3.

29 Ibid.

30 Ibid.

31 Ibid.

32 Ibid.

33 Ibid., January 8, 1879, 3.

34 Ibid., August 1, 1879, 3.

35 Ibid., July 9, 1880, 2.

36 Ibid., August 1, 1879, 3.

37 Ibid., January 8, 1879, 3.

38 Ibid., May 2, 1879, 2.

39 Ibid., March 19, 1879, 3.

40 Ibid., August 1, 1879, 3.

41 Ibid.

42 Ibid.

43 *Memorial Record of the Northern Peninsula of Michigan* (Chicago: The Lewis Publishing Company, 1895).

44 *Gladwin County Record*, August 1, 1879, 3.

45 Ibid.

46 Ibid., November 19, 1878, 3.

47 Ibid., January 15, 1879, 3.

48 Ibid., December 18, 1878, 3.

49 Ibid., February 26, 1879, 3.

50 Ibid., February 5, 1879, 3.

CHAPTER 5. Mr. Nester's Army

1 *Federal Census 1880* (Michigan, Roscommon County, Nester Township, Enumeration District 288), 1-5.

CHAPTER 6. Nester Settles In

1 *Gladwin County Record*, July 9, 1880, 2.

2 Ibid., September 10, 1880, 3.

3 Ibid.

4   Ibid., December 5, 1879, 3.
5   Ibid., August 19, 1881, 3.
6   Ibid.
7   Ibid., August 11, 1882, 3.
8   Ibid., July 9, 1880, 2.
9   Ibid., August 19, 1881, 3.
10 Ibid., May 20, 1881, 3.
11 Ibid., August 19, 1881, 3.
12 Ibid., April 23, 1880, 3.
13 Ibid., February 27, 1880, 3.
14 Ibid., January 7, 1881, 3.
15 Ibid., June 17, 1881, 2.
16 Ibid., July 9, 1880, 2.
17 Ibid., June 20, 1879, 3.
18 Ibid., January 16, 1880, 3.
19 Ibid., February 27, 1880, 3.
20 Ibid., December 3, 1880, 3.
21 Ibid., March 11, 1881, 3.
22 Ibid., April 23, 1880, 3.
23 Ibid., May 2, 1879, 2.
24 Ibid., July 9, 1880, 2.
25 Ibid., April 23, 1880, 3.
26 Ibid., September 10, 1880, 3.
27 Ibid., September 9, 1881, 3.
28 Ibid.
29 Ibid., July 30, 1880, 3.
30 Ibid., May 20, 1881, 3.
31 Ibid., August 19, 1881, 3.
32 Ibid., December 2, 1881, 2.
33 Ibid., February 18, 1881, 3.
34 Ibid., July 11, 1879, 3.
35 Ibid., March 19, 1880, 2.
36 Ibid., May 28, 1880, 3.
37 Ibid., September 10, 1880, 3.
38 Ibid., April 23, 1880, 3.
39 Ibid., December 5, 1879, 3.
40 Ibid., April 16, 1880, 3.
41 Ibid., May 6, 1881, 3.
42 *American Engineer,* Vol. 5, No.5, Friday, February 2, 1883, 62.
43 *Gladwin County Record*, April 23, 1880, 3.
44 Ibid., July 9, 1880, 2.

CHAPTER 7. The Big Sale

1   *Portrait and Biographical Album of the Members of the Legislature of the State of Michigan, 1883* (Chicago: Chapman Brothers, 1883).
2   *Gladwin County Record*, August 20, 1880, 3.
3   Ibid., March 18, 1881, 3.
4   Ibid., September 23, 1881, 3.
5   Ibid., November 18, 1881, 3.
6   Ibid., December 2, 1881, 2.
7   Ibid.
8   Ibid.
9   Ibid., December 30, 1881, 3.
10 Ibid., January 6, 1882, 3.
11 Land Transfer Records, Roscommon County Clerk's Office, Roscommon, Michigan.
12 *Gladwin County Record*, January 6, 1882, 3.
13 Land Transfer Records, Roscommon County Clerk's Office, Roscommon, Michigan.
14 *Gladwin County Record*, January 6, 1882, 3.

CHAPTER 8. Wright, Wells, and Stone Take Over

1   *Gladwin County Record*, July 28, 1882, 3.
2   Ibid., January 12, 1883, 3.
3   Ibid., April 21, 1882, 2.
4   Ibid., June 30, 1882, 3.
5   Ibid., July 14, 1882, 3.
6   Ibid., July 21, 1882, 3.
7   Ibid., December 22, 1882, 3.
8   Ibid.
9   Ibid., January 12, 1883, 3.
10 Ibid., July 6, 1883, 2.
11 Ibid., November 2, 1883, 5.
12 Ibid., January 11, 1884, 5.
13 Ibid., March 14, 1884, 1.
14 Ibid., April 18, 1884, 5.
15 Ibid., June 27, 1884, 1.
16 Ibid., August 15, 1884, 1.
17 Ibid., December 26, 1884, 1.
18 Ibid., October 31, 1884, 5.
19 *Record of the Appointments of Postmasters, 1832–Sept. 30 1971, Mich.,* Volume 54, ca. 1878-96 (National Archives, Copy, State Library of Michigan).

20 *Gladwin County Record*, November 7, 1884, 1.

21 Ibid., December 5, 1884, 5.

22 Ibid., November 7, 1884, 3.

23 Ibid., August 7, 1885, 5.

24 Ibid., August 21, 1885, 5.

25 Ibid., August 28, 1885, 5.

26 Ibid., August 18, 1893, 1.

CHAPTER 9. The Roscommon Lumber Company

1   Hiram Carleton, *Genealogical and Family History of the State of Vermont, A Record of the Achievements of Her People in the Making of a Commonwealth and the Founding of a Nation. Vol. II* (New York & Chicago: The Lewis Publishing Company, 1903).

2   *Gladwin County Record*, May 19, 1882, 3.

3   Ibid., April 16, 1886, 1.

4   *Muskegon Daily Chronicle*, February 9, 1884, 2.

5   George W. Hotchkiss, *History of the Lumber and Forest Industry of the Northwest* (Chicago: George W. Hotchkiss & Co., 1898).

6   Hiram Carleton, *Genealogical and Family History of the State of Vermont, A Record of the Achievements of Her People in the Making of a Commonwealth and the Founding of a Nation. Vol. II* (New York & Chicago: The Lewis Publishing Company, 1903).

7   *Gladwin County Record*, May 19, 1882, 3.

8   *Lumberman's Gazette*, May 24, 1882, 5.

9   *Gladwin County Record*, March 16, 1883, 3.

10 Robertson Howard, ed., *The Northwestern Reporter*, 26 (St. Paul: West Publishing Company, 1886).

11 *Industrial Chicago, The Building Interests* (Chicago: The Goodspeed Publishing Company, 1891).

12 Ibid.

13 W. B. Judson, *Lumber Statistics and Logging Railroads of the Northwest* (Chicago: W. B. Judson, Publisher, 1885).

14 *Lumberman's Gazette*, January 24, 1883, 4.

15 John W. Fitzmaurice, *"The Shanty Boy," or Life in a Lumber Camp* (Berrien Springs, Michigan: Hardscrabble Books, 1979).

16 *Muskegon Daily Chronicle*, February 5, 1884, 3.

17 Ibid., December 30, 1884, 2.

18 Ibid., May 16, 1883, 4.

19 *The Roscommon News*, April 22, 1887, 4.

20 *Gladwin County Record*, April 16, 1886, 1.

21 Ibid., April 30, 1886, 1.

22   Ibid., May 13, 1887, 5.

23   Ibid.

24   Ibid., July 29, 1887, 5.

25   Ibid., June 22, 1888, 1.

26   *The Northwestern Reporter*, 44 (St. Paul: West Publishing Co., 1890).

27   *Gladwin County Record*, October 18, 1889, 5.

28   Hiram Carleton, *Genealogical and Family History of the State of Vermont, A Record of the Achievements of Her People in the Making of a Commonwealth and the Founding of a Nation. Vol. II* (New York & Chicago: The Lewis Publishing Company, 1903).

29   *The Roscommon News*, January 4, 1889, 8.

CHAPTER 10. The Last Train to Edna

1   *Gladwin County Record*, December 24, 1880, 3.

2   Ibid., August 17, 1883, 1.

3   Ibid., October 26, 1883, 5.

4   David M. Ellis, *Michigan Postal History, The Post Offices, 1805–1986* (Lake Grove, Oregon: The Depot, 1993).

5   *Gladwin County Record*, November 16, 1883, 5.

6   Ibid., December 9, 1887, 1.

7   Ibid., July 18, 1884, 5.

8   Ibid., June 23, 1885, 1.

9   Ibid., August 28, 1885, 5.

10   Ibid., April 16, 1886, 1.

11   Ibid., June 25, 1886, 8.

12   Ibid., July 23, 1886, 1.

13   Ibid., May 27, 1887, 5.

14   Ibid., July 22, 1887, 5.

CHAPTER 11. The State Count

1   *Michigan State Census 1884* (Roscommon County, Nester Township), 1-20.

CHAPTER 12. The Railroad from the East

1   Perry F. Powers, *A History of Northern Michigan and its People. Vol. I* (Chicago: The Lewis Publishing Company, 1912).

2   *Gladwin County Record*, October 5, 1883, 5.

3   Ibid., July 25, 1884, 1.

4   Ibid., September 5, 1884, 5.

5   Ibid., September 9, 1887, 5.

6   Ibid., November 4, 1887, 5.

7   Ibid., December 21, 1888, 5.

8   Ibid., August 1, 1890, 4.

9   Land Transfer Records, Roscommon County Clerk's Office, Roscommon, Michigan.

10 *Gladwin County Record*, October 17, 1890, 5.

11 Ibid., January 30, 1891, 5.

CHAPTER 13. The Clear Lake Harvest

1   *Gladwin County Record*, April 15, 1892, 1.

2   *The Roscommon News*, July 8, 1892, 8.

3   *Gladwin County Record*, June 30, 1893, 1.

4   Ibid., August 18, 1893, 5.

5   Ibid., October 6, 1893, 4.

6   Ibid., June 15, 1894, 4.

7   Ibid., August 3, 1894, 1-2.

8   Ibid., August 31, 1894, 7.

9   Ibid., September 28, 1894, 2.

10 Ibid., August 16, 1895, 7.

11 Ibid., December 6, 1895, 5.

12 Ibid., October 4, 1895, 5.

13 Ibid., December 6, 1895, 5.

14 Ibid., October 4, 1895, 5.

15 Ibid., January 31, 1896, 1.

16 Ibid., April 10, 1896, 4.

17 Ibid., June 12, 1896, 5.

18 Ibid., September 4, 1896, 5.

19 Land Transfer Records, Roscommon County Clerk's Office, Roscommon, Michigan.

20 *The Roscommon News*, July 8, 1892, 8.

21 Land Transfer Records, Roscommon County Clerk's Office, Roscommon, Michigan.

22 *Gladwin County Record*, April 30, 1897, 5.

23 Ibid., December 23, 1898, 1.

CHAPTER 14. Pernicious Pines

1   *Gladwin County Record*, March 12, 1880, 1.

2   Ibid., January 18, 1884, 5.

3   Ibid., March 21, 1884, 5.

4   Ibid., August 10, 1883, 1.

5   Ibid., February 25, 1881, 3.

6   Ibid., April 22, 1881, 3.

7   Ibid., June 6, 1884, 1.

8   Ibid., October 16, 1885, 5.

9   Ibid., January 1, 1886, 5.

10 Ibid., March 12, 1886, 5.

11 Ibid., June 4, 1886, 1.

12 Ibid., December 24, 1886, 5.

13 Ibid., December 7, 1888, 5.

14 Ibid., April 22, 1881, 3.

15 Ibid., December 27, 1889, 5.

16 Ibid., January 16, 1880, 3.

CHAPTER 15. Lally's Wye

1   J. F. Pratt. Boyce Lines, Hauptman Branch. Railroad construction map. February 1896. Boyce Lumber Company Records. Box 7. Clarke Historical Library, Central Michigan University, Mount Pleasant, MI.

2   R. Meister & Sons. Letter to: Jonathan Boyce. 1893 June 15. Boyce Lumber Company Records. Box 13. Clarke Historical Library, Central Michigan University, Mount Pleasant, MI.

3   *Gladwin County Record*, June 2, 1893, 5.

4   Ibid., June 2, 1899, 8.

CHAPTER 16. Old Nolan

1   National Archives, Records Group 28: Records of the Post Office Department, 1773-1950, Series: Report of Site Locations, 1837-1950, File Unit: Michigan: Ontonagon-Roscommon, p. 1011-12.

2   Ibid.

3   *Record of the Appointments of Postmasters, 1832–Sept. 30 1971, Mich.,* Volume 54, ca. 1878-96 (National Archives, Copy, State Library of Michigan).

4   *The Roscommon News*, March 6, 1896, 1.

5   Ibid.

6   Ibid.

7   *Gladwin County Record*, March 13, 1896, 5.

8   Ibid., December 13, 1895, 4.

9   Ibid., January 17, 1896, 5.

10 Ibid., December 20, 1895, 5.

11 Ibid., February 28, 1986, 1.

12 *The Roscommon Herald*, January 27, 1893, 8.

13 *Gladwin Country Record*, April 6, 1894, 5.

14 Ibid., November 8, 1895, 8.

CHAPTER 17. The Actress, the General, and the Lawyer

1 T. Allison Brown, *A History of the New York Stage from the First Performance in 1732 to 1901*. Vol. II (New York: Dodd, Mead and Company, 1903).

2 *The New York Times*, February 26, 1895, Part One, 8.

3 *History of Milwaukee City and County. Vol. II* (Chicago-Milwaukee: The S. J. Clarke Publishing Company, 1922).

CHAPTER 18. The Central Michigan Land Company

1 *Gladwin County Record*, July 31, 1903, 7.

2 *National Magazine* XXI, no. 6, March 1905.

3 *Gladwin County Record*, October 27, 1910, 1.

CHAPTER 19. The Commission Merchant

1 A.T. Andreas, *History of Chicago. From the Earliest Period to the Present Time. Vol. III* (Chicago: The A.T. Andreas Co., 1886).

2 *Chicago Daily Tribune*, August 3, 1893, 1.

3 *The Indianapolis Journal*, August 3, 1893, 5.

4 *Chicago Daily Tribune*, May 19, 1919, 17.

5 *The Indianapolis Journal*, August 3, 1893, 5.

6 Ibid.

7 *Chicago Daily Tribune*, August 2, 1893, 1.

8 Ibid., August 3, 1893, 1.

9 *Industrial Chicago. Vol. IV, The Commercial Interests* (Chicago: The Goodspeed Publishing Company, 1894).

10 Ibid.

11 *Chicago Daily Tribune*, January 5, 1894, 5.

12 Ibid., March 10, 1897, 1.

CHAPTER 20. The Brothers Thomas

1 *Medical Era. Vol. XIX* (Chicago Era Publishing Company, 1901).

2 Ibid.

3 Ibid.

4 *Gladwin County Record*, April 16, 1914, 5.

5 Ibid., May 27, 1915, 1.

6 Ibid., March 29, 1917, 5.

7 Ibid., April 19, 1917, 1.

CHAPTER 21. Destructive Distillation

1   Perry F. Powers, *A History of Northern Michigan and its People. Vol I* (Chicago: The Lewis Publishing Company, 1912).

2   *Paint, Oil and Drug Review* 48, no. 10 (March 6, 1907): 24.

3   *The Northwestern Reporter (annotated). Vol. 120* (St Paul: West Publishing Co., 1909).

4   Ibid.

5   Ibid.

6   *Paint, Oil and Drug Review* 51, no. 14 (April 5, 1911): 26.

7   *The Northwestern Reporter (annotated). Vol. 120* (St Paul: West Publishing Co., 1909).

8   *Gladwin County Record*, March 14, 1907, 1.

9   *Paint, Oil and Drug Review* 43, no. 5 (January 30, 1907): 3.

10   *Gladwin County Record*, March 14, 1907, 1.

11   *Paint, Oil and Drug Review* 43, no. 5 (January 30, 1907): 3.

12   *State of Michigan. Twenty-Fifth Annual Report of the Bureau of Labor and Statistics* (Lansing, MI: Wynkoop Hallenbeck Crawford Co., State Printers, 1908).

13   *State of Michigan. Twenty-Sixth Annual Report of the Bureau of Labor and Statistics* (Lansing, MI: Wynkoop Hallenbeck Crawford Co., State Printers, 1909).

14   *Gladwin County Record*, September 16, 1909, 1.

15   Ibid., June 18, 1908, 1.

16   Ibid., October 27, 1910, 1.

17   Ibid., March 13, 1974, section B, 1.

18   Ibid., August 11, 1910, 7.

19   Ibid., June 6, 1912, 5.

20   Ibid., March 5, 1914, 6.

21   *Roscommon Herald-News*, February 20, 1919, 5.

CHAPTER 22. The Milwaukee Fruit Farm

1   *Gladwin County Record*, June 6, 1912, 5.

2   Ibid., October 13, 1905, 5.

3   Ibid., March 14, 1907, 1.

4   Ibid., March 13, 1974, section B, 1.

5   Ibid., October 27, 1910, 1.

6   Ibid., September 28, 1911, 4.

7   Ibid., September 12, 1918, 8.

8   Ibid., October 24, 1918, 5.

9   Ibid., July 28, 1910, 8.

10   Ibid., September 29, 1910, 7.

11 Ibid., May 3, 1917, 6.

12 Ibid., December 16, 1917, 4.

13 Ibid., October 13, 1921, 3.

14 Ibid., October 27, 1927, 3.

15 Ibid., December 7, 1911, 5.

16 Ibid., November 14, 1912, 8.

17 Ibid., May 13, 1920, 3.

18 Ibid., December 4, 1919, 2.

19 Ibid., December 11, 1919, 2.

20 Ibid., March 29, 1920, 8.

21 Ibid., May 6, 1920, 6.

22 Ibid., October 27, 1921, 3.

23 Ibid., December 22, 1921, 3.

CHAPTER 23. Social Milieu, Charivari, etc.

1 *Gladwin County Record*, September 26, 1907, 6.

2 Personal communication, James A. Kimble, June 13, 2011.

3 *Federal Census 1910* (Michigan, Roscommon County, Nester Township, Sheet 3A).

4 *Gladwin County Record*, February 27, 1908, 8.

5 Ibid., December 17, 1908, 7.

6 Ibid., April 9, 1908, 8.

7 Ibid., April 30, 1908, 7.

8 Ibid., April 23, 1908, 8.

9 Ibid., June 23, 1921, 7.

10 Ibid., November 28, 1907, 8.

11 Ibid., December 17, 1908, 7.

12 Ibid., July 11, 1907, 8.

13 Ibid., December 5, 1907, 8.

14 Ibid., October 17, 1907, 8.

15 Ibid., August 25, 1910, 7.

16 Ibid., January 12, 1911, 7.

17 Ibid., December 18, 1919, 2.

CHAPTER 24. Buildings

1 *Gladwin County Record*, March 13, 1974, section B, 1.

2 Ibid., March 20, 1974, section B, 9.

3 Ibid., October 17, 1907, 8.

CHAPTER 25. Some Unpolished Verse

1 *Gladwin County Record*, January 16, 1908, 8.

CHAPTER 26. Badger, Verncroft, and the Riddle of Jacwac

1 *Gladwin County Record*, September 16, 1909, 1.
2 Walter Romig, *Michigan Place Names* (Detroit: Wayne State University Press, 1986).
3 *Roscommon Herald*, April 14, 1910, 4.
4 *Gladwin County Record*, October 20, 1910, 5.
5 Walter Romig, *Michigan Place Names* (Detroit: Wayne State University Press, 1986).
6 *Gladwin County Record*, February 1, 1923, 5.
7 *Plat Book of Roscommon Co.*, Mich. (Rockford, Ill.: W.W. Hixson & Co., believed to be published between 1930 and 1939).
8 David M. Ellis, *Michigan Postal History, The Post Offices, 1805–1986* (Lake Grove, Oregon: The Depot, 1993).

CHAPTER 27. Taking Up the Last Steel

1 *Gladwin County Record*, June 2, 1899, 8.
2 *Gladwin County Record*, December 15, 1899, 5.
3 *The Roscommon News*, September 11, 1905, 8.
4 Ibid., August 30, 1907, 1.
5 *Gladwin County Record*, February 11, 1909, 5.
6 *Roscommon Herald*, August 12, 1909, 5.
7 *Gladwin County Record*, August 25, 1910, 5.
8 Ibid., October 27, 1910, 1.
9 *Roscommon Herald*, November 3, 1910, 4.
10 *Gladwin County Record*, June 6, 1912, 5.

CHAPTER 28. 1910 Census and Constraints

1 Federal Census 1910, Michigan, Roscommon County, Nester Township, Enumeration District 185, Sheet Numbers 2A, 2B, 3A.
2 *Gladwin County Record*, October 27, 1910, 1.
3 Ibid., July 28, 1910, 8.
4 Ibid., September 29, 1910, 7.
5 Ibid., September 15, 1910, 8.

Chapter 29. Charles B. Eggleston vs. the Central Michigan Land Co.

1 Charles B. Eggleston vs. Central Michigan Land Co et al, Civil Case 209, Filed 5/29/1913, 34th Circuit Court, Roscommon, Michigan.
2 *Gladwin County Record*, June 6, 1912, 5.
3 Charles B. Eggleston vs. Central Michigan Land Co et al, Civil Case 209, Filed 5/29/1913, 34th Circuit Court, Roscommon, Michigan.
4 Land Transfer Records, Roscommon County Clerk's Office, Roscommon, Michigan.

Chapter 30. False and Fraudulent Representation

1 Mary Eggleston vs. C. B. Hillman, Kay McKay, George R. Smith and Emile Franklin Pierce, Civil Case 262, Filed 2/10/1919, 34th Circuit Court, Roscommon, Michigan.

Chapter 31. The School Teacher

1 Wellesley College. *Wellesley college record*, 1875–1912.
2 *Federal Census 1870*, Illinois, Cook County, 12th Ward of the City of Chicago: 195.
3 *Gladwin County Record*, June 12, 1940, 5.
4 Passport Applications, January 2, 1906–March 31,1925; General Records of the Department of State, Record Group 59; National Archives, Washington, D.C.
5 Passenger and Crew Lists of Vessels Arriving at New York, New York, 1897–1957; Records of the Immigration and Naturalization service; National Archives, Washington, D.C.
6 *Gladwin County Record*, November 14, 1912, 8.
7 Federal Census 1920, Arizona, Maricopa County, Phoenix, Precinct 2, Sheet Number 5A.
8 John C. Porter, *Mid-Forest Lodge* (Private Publication, 1969).
9 *Gladwin County Record*, October 1, 1925, 1.
10 Ibid.
11 Ibid., May 14, 1925, 4.
12 *Detroit Free Press*, September 27, 1925, part 5, 5.
13 Ibid.
14 Ibid.
15 *Gladwin County Record*, October 1, 1925, 1.
16 Ibid., July 5, 1923, 8.
17 Land Transfer Records, Roscommon County Clerk's Office, Roscommon, Michigan.

18 *Detroit Free Press*, October 22, 1935, 22.

19 *Gladwin County Record*, April 22, 1926, 4.

20 Ibid., October 18, 1928, 4.

21 Ibid., June 12, 1940, 5.

22 *Federal Census 1930*, California, Los Angeles County, Pasadena, Enumeration District 19-1243, Sheet Number 15A.

23 Candace L. Campbell, *A Brief History of The Shakespeare Club* (Private Publication, 2019).

24 Personal Communication, Candace L. Campbell, Historian, Shakespeare Club of Pasadena, February 13, 2021.

25 *Gladwin County Record*, June 12, 1940, 5.

26 Land Transfer Records, Roscommon County Clerk's Office, Roscommon, Michigan.

27 *Gladwin County Record*, June 12, 1940, 5.

Chapter 32. Native Son

1 *Federal Census 1870*, Michigan, Genesee County, Township of Fenton, Page No. 26.

2 *Federal Census 1880*, Michigan, Crawford County, Maple Forest, p. 1.

3 Ibid.

4 General Land Office of the United States, Homestead Certificate No. 1647, January 9,1886.

5 *Federal Census 1900*, Michigan, Crawford County, Township of Maple Forest, Sheet No. 2.

6 *Federal Census 1910*, Michigan, Roscommon County, Roscommon Township, Sheet No. 7B.

7 State of Michigan, Local Acts of the Legislature of the State of Michigan passed at the Regular Session of 1913 (Lansing: Wynkoop Hallenbeck Crawford Co., 1913).

8 State of Michigan, Proceedings of the Public Domain Commission, Vol. VII 1915-16 (Lansing: Wynkoop Hallenbeck Crawford Co., 1916).

9 *Detroit Free Press*, February 2, 1919, 18.

10 Michigan Cattle & Sheep Ranch Co., Ranching in Michigan, Presented by the Northeastern Michigan Development Bureau, 1919.

11 *Federal Census 1920*, Michigan, Roscommon County, Lake Township, Sheet No. 3B.

12 Roy L. Dodge, *Michigan Ghost Towns. Vol. II* (Troy, Michigan; Glendon Publishing, 1971).

13 *Federal Census 1930*, Michigan, Roscommon County, Lake Township, Sheet No. 1A.

14 *Gobles News*, June 30, 1927, 4.

15   *Lansing State Journal*, January 6, 1931, 2.

16   *Escanaba Daily Press*, August 9, 1930, 13.

17   John C. Porter, *Mid-Forest Lodge* (Private Publication, 1969).

18   Ibid.

19   Michigan Divorce Records, 1897–1952, Roscommon County, Docket No. 641, 1941.

20   Michigan Marriage Records, 1867–1952, Roscommon County, No. 977, 1941.

Chapter 33. Passing the Baton

1   Land Transfer Records, Roscommon County Clerk's Office, Roscommon, Michigan.

Chapter 34. Green Gold

1   Rolland H. Maybee, *Michigan's White Pine Era* (Lansing, Michigan: Michigan History Division, Michigan Department of State, 1976).

2   *Saginaw Courier-Herald*, May 13, 1890, 2.

3   Herbert Nolan, *In Memory of THE CAMP SIXTEENERS* (Sanford, Michigan, 1970).

4   *Compendium of History and Biography of the City of Detroit and Wayne County, Michigan* (Chicago: Henry Taylor & Co., 1909).

5   *The Daily Mining Journal* (Marquette, MI): May 12, 1890, 8.

6   James Cooke Mills, *History of Saginaw County Michigan, Volume II* (Saginaw: Seemann & Peters Publishers, 1918).

7   Wayne County Michigan Probate Packet 15877, 1890.

8   *Star Tribune* (Minneapolis, MN): October 30, 1893, 5.

9   *Detroit Free Press*, October 26, 1893, 3.

10   *Star Tribune* (Minneapolis, MN): October 20, 1893, 1.

11   James Cooke Mills, *History of Saginaw County Michigan, Volume II* (Saginaw: Seemann & Peters Publishers, 1918).

12   *Detroit Free Press*, December 6, 1893, 3.

13   *Star Tribune* (Minneapolis, MN): December 6, 1893, 1.

14   George W. Hotchkiss, *History of the Lumber and Forest Industry of the Northwest* (Chicago: George W. Hotchkiss & Co., 1898).

15   Public Officials of Chicago, 1895–1896, The Municipal Herald of Chicago containing a portraiture of Public Officials of the city of Chicago (Chicago: John C Sterchie, publisher, 1896).

16   John Bersey, *Cyclopedia of Michigan* (New York and Detroit: Western Publishing and Engraving, 1900).

17   Ibid.

18 James Cooke Mills, *History of Saginaw County Michigan, Volume II* (Saginaw: Seemann & Peters Publishers, 1918).

19 David McMacken, *Built on Pines, The Story of Ammi Willard Wright* (Alma, MI: The Alma Public Library, 2003).

20 *St. Louis Post-Dispatch* (St. Louis, MO): February 23, 1897, 4.

21 *Decatur Daily Republican* (Decatur, IL): June 1, 1893, 3.

22 *The Marion Star* (Marion, OH) March 16, 1914, 3.

23 *Star Tribune* (Minneapolis, MN): December 6, 1893, 1.

24 Ibid.

25 George W. Hotchkiss, *Industrial Chicago, The Lumber Interest* (Chicago: The Goodspeed Publishing Company, 1894).

AUTHOR'S NOTE

1 *The Mining Journal* (Marquette, MI), April 12, 1902, 4.

ABOUT THE AUTHOR

Thomas Schupbach has had a lifelong interest in Michigan history. He has co-authored numerous articles in *Michigan History Magazine* and the *Chronicle,* a quarterly publication of the Historical Society of Michigan. Tom is active in land conservation issues and is on the board of a regional Land Conservancy. He enjoys a wide range of outdoor activities and resides in Northern Michigan.

www.ingramcontent.com/pod-product-compliance
Lightning Source LLC
Chambersburg PA
CBHW070921120626

46546CB00001B/357

9 781961 302105